RURAL VULNERABILITY TO FAMINE IN ETHIOPIA

D1727531

Rural vulnerability to famine in Ethiopia - 1958-1977

Mesfin Wolde Mariam

INTERMEDIATE TECHNOLOGY PUBLICATIONS
1986

Published by Intermediate Technology Publications Ltd,
9 King Street, London WC2E 8HW, U.K.

© Intermediate Technology Publications, 1986

ISBN 0 946688 03 6

Printed in Great Britain by A. Wheaton & Co Ltd, Exeter

Contents

Preface

It is a paradoxical fact that I was introduced to famine by Weizero Ghennet Wolde-Gabriel; paradoxical, because Weizero Ghennet is a lady who does not ostensibly have any reason to know famine, let alone introduce it effectively to a man who, because of his very modest background, has every reason to know famine. The Amharic language has two different words for the English word "rich" or "wealthy". One is *habtam*, which simply means one who possesses wealth; and the other is *baletsega*. The word *baletsega* literally means one who possesses grace, and the implication is, I believe, that *baletsega* is different from *habtam* in the sense that, although both words indicate wealth, *habtam* remains material and personal, while *baletsega* is endowed not only with material wealth but also with grace and through it with a consciousness of social responsibility. It appears that, while wealth for the *habtam* is the means of personal gratification, for the *baletsega* it goes much beyond, to become an instrument of manifesting social responsibility as trustees of God who is believed to be the source of grace. Weizero Ghennet was a *baletsega* in that sense of the word.

In 1958 when practically nobody amidst the pleasures of Addis Ababa knew anything about the famine that was killing thousands of people in Tigray, Weizero Ghennet was carrying on a one-person relief aid. Quite obviously the magnitude of the famine at that time in Tigray would have been too much even for the government of Ethiopia, had it decided to accept the responsibility. Weizero Ghennet's effort compared to the magnitude of the problem may be considered a drop in the ocean. But not only did she constantly send money, food and clothes to the victims of famine in Tigray, but she also devoted her energy and time to make people aware of the sufferings of people, a kind of suffering that she was fortunate enough not to have even remotely experienced or witnessed. It was only her social consciousness and vivid imagination that allowed her, or even obliged her, to come to a total realization of the problem. Nobody that went to her house at any time left without knowing about the seriousness of the famine in Tigray.

To be informed and to know may very often only lead to a purely momentary concern that is expressed by the traditional Ethiopian lip-sucking gesture, and may not lead to any realization of the problem, let alone to any action. It was, nevertheless, only during visits to her house that I became aware of the famine in Tigray. It took several visits for me to be convinced of the seriousness of the problem and to make an effort to know more about the Tigray Famine. So I took the bus to Tigray and saw for myself the horrible face of famine.

It was an unforgettable sight, one too horrible to describe. I returned with a very deep sense of shame and a decision to do something about it, although I was not sure exactly what I could do. Even the fact that American relief grain was being distributed, or maldistributed, did not come out as a news item. I wrote a short description of the famine and tried to have it printed in the newspapers. It was impossible. Through the university and the Toastmasters Club, whatever possible was done to spread the horrible news of the famine in Tigray. At the same time, an attempt was made to form a relief committee and to have it recognized by the government. After much effort and many discussions with high-ranking government officials, it proved to be impossible, mainly because the one person who alone could decide on the issue was on a State Visit in the USSR. It was impossible even to find people to work with in organizing relief operations without prior approval of the government. But then, when the Emperor returned from the USSR, a description of the famine with two photographs and the urgent need for relief aid was submitted to him. Partly, perhaps, to short-circuit the effort for establishing a relief committee, and partly, perhaps, to respond to my own letter, a letter,from the Ministry of Pen, which means "by order of the Emperor", sent me back to Tigray—to distribute, together with other people "20,000" quintals of grain which the Emperor "graciously" donated. In one month, a long and terribly gruelling month, during which, day and night, one saw and heard the agonies of starved women and children, only about one-quarter of the promised amount of grain arrived. Most of the time it was a rough waiting, waiting that hurt even us, let alone the starving multitudes from Maichew to Meqele to Addigrat to Axum and Adwa. Finally, when the waiting became unbearable, I unloaded the agony on the shoulder of the more patient and efficient companion, Mulugheta Ghebre-Wold, and left for Addis Ababa to bury my herd in the sand of illusion. Upon my return to Addis Ababa I submitted a report to the Ministry of Interior describing the terrible condition of the victims, the delay and the inadequacy of the relief aid, and the uselessness of distributing grain instead of ready-made food.

The ghastly scene of famine left its indelible imprint on my mind. That experience convinced me personally of the urgent need to do something about famine. But the fact that I could not even have the description of the famine in Tigray printed in any of the newspapers, together with the long delay in delivering relief aid to the victims, cast a shadow of doubt in my mind, a doubt whether famine is really a consequence of natural phenomena such as drought or locust invasion, or whether it is the failure of the socio-economic and political system. Certainly, if there were more people like Weizero Ghennet, more lives could be saved, but the problem could not be eliminated. At any rate, no society, least of all that of Ethiopia, can have as many such persons as it requires to avert famine. And even if there were the requisite number of such people, it would still be necessary to organize them in order to make them effective. Such an organization was impossible without the active participation and support of the government.

Subsequent events confirmed my feeling that natural phenomena have less to do with famine than society itself and its various institutions. This study, therefore, is the outcome of the doubts and questions that have been lingering in my mind since 1958. By sheer coincidence the archives of the Ministry of Interior have files on famine beginning the year of 1958. That is why the time is limited to twenty years, starting in 1958 and ending in 1977, when the preliminary investigation of this study started.

This study is organized into five parts. Part One, the Introduction, attempts to define the conceptual framework of the study as a whole. Part Two, which includes two chapters, deals with the problem of famine as well as its consequences. Part Three, which also includes two chapters discusses the socio-economic and political conditions that create vulnerability to famine. Part Four, which again consists of two chapters, is an attempt to show, on one hand, the deficiencies in the conventional explanations of famine, and, on the other, to demonstrate a new analysis and a new explanation of famine. Part Five, the Conclusion, deals mainly with suggestions and recommendations for eradicating the threat of famine from Ethiopia.

MESFIN WOLDE MARIAM

Acknowledgements

The study started with a modest fund provided by the Addis Ababa University and the active cooperation of the Institute of Development Research. Later on, Clark University, Massachusetts, USA, provided additional funds to enable this study to proceed at an accelerated rate. Clark University also provided certain facilities which expedited preliminary investigation. To these Institutions I am very grateful. I must especially mention Dr. Richard Ford and Dr. Len Berry of Clark University for their valuable assistance and encouragement.

Within Ethiopia, I am indebted to the Ministry of Interior, the Central Statistical Office, the Relief and Rehabilitation Commission, and the Ethiopian Nutrition Institute for their cooperation in providing various data and information. In spite of very difficult circumstances, Dr. Duri Mohammed, President of Addis Ababa University, together with his administrative staff, did his best to help me finish this research project; Dr. Alula Abate, Director of Institute of Development Research, provided basic support; Dr. Shibru Tedla, the Research Officer, provided some financial assistance for secretarial work. Dr. Alemayehu Haile (Mathematics Department) and Dr. Asme rom Kidane (Statistics Department), of Addis Ababa University, have guided and helped me greatly with the statistical aspect of this study, and I owe them special gratitude. In this connection I also acknowledge with thanks the critical remarks and valuable suggestions of Dr. Ayenew Ijigu (Statistics Department, A.A.U.). Mr. G. Lardner (ECA), Dr. Bekure Wolde-Semait (Department of Geography, A.A.U.), and Dr. Abraham Besrat (Graduate School, A.A.U.) read the manuscript and made valuable suggestions; to all three I am grateful. Needless to say, I alone am responsible for whatever weaknesses may be detected in this study.

Finally I must thank all those who helped me with the seemingly endless calculation of masses of data, as well as Weizerit Haimanot Dejene who patiently typed draft after draft. To Herbert C. Heidt and his staff at Clark University I express my deep gratitude for the maps they made, although final alterations made it impossible to use them. For the cartographic work I am indebted to Weizero Tsedale-Mariam Bayu.

To Weizero Ghennet Wolde-Gabriel
and
to the Young Mother of Tigray
Who, from opposite extremes, demonstrated the contagious
Pain of Famine

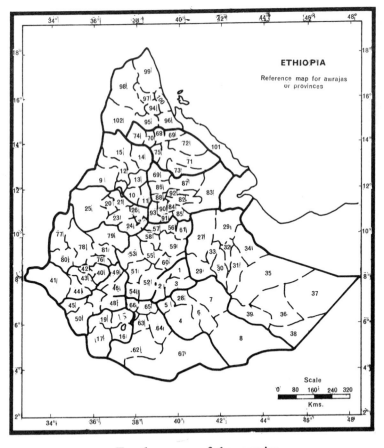

For the names of the *awrajas,*
refer to the code numbers in Table XX (pp. 171-73).

PART I

INTRODUCTION

Chapter One

Introduction

Famine creates a disturbing scene. To witness the agony, degradation, hopelessness and silent anger on the dismal and skeletal faces, on one hand, and on the other hand, to see the articulated or unarticulated faith for survival while in the agony of slow and grinding teeth of famine; to see the slender and uncontrollable hope for miraculous succour in the face of pious indifference; to see the confidence in the society and its leaders in spite of evidence only to the contrary; and above all, to see the serene dignity and sense of decorum of the starving shocks one out of the illusion of higher values in human life and creates a double sense of utter shame: first, it is a parochial sense of shame of belonging to a society that allows the process of famine to go through its full course—several months of journey to death; and secondly, it is a universal sense of shame of belonging to humanity, that with all its lofty self-image, grand ideals, and impressive achievements, has not yet solved the most elementary problem of food supply.

Famine is a visible horror. The fortunate part of mankind may have only heard or read about famine. They may have even seen it on the screen. None of this second-hand learning can match the reality of famine, the actual sight of emaciated human beings struggling against premature death. The magnitude of the problem together with the intensity of the suffering permeates one's conscience to make the normal three meals a day a pain of guilt. How does any society allow its own members to be straved to death when some are overstuffing themselves with food? In fact can we really talk of a *society* under circumstances in which periodic mass death by starvation is the lot of the majority? Is famine not the most concrete manifestation of the alienation and dispensability of the mass? Is not famine a demonstration of class division, as well as a proof of the indifference of the ruling class to the misery and suffering of the masses?

Nothing else manifests man's inhumanity to man more than famine. Nothing else expresses the hypocrisy of cultural and religious values. Nothing else shatters the myth of social and political unity. Nothing else reveals social, economic and political anarchy more than famine. When conditions are relatively normal and when the masses of peasants have some capacity to produce, the iron law that everybody must contribute to the common good operates with harsh constancy. But when, under extremely adverse circumstances, the masses of peasants starve to death, the mechanism of the common good that normally serves to rationalize the exploitation of the masses of poor peasants breaks down totally and leaves them in helpless disarray. This fact forces us to question the values and institutions of a society that allows its members to die of famine. To reduce the problem of famine to natural factors or to raise it to international conspiracy of some sort is to miss the centre of the issue and to exonerate the values and institutions that, both by omission and commission, play a direct role in promoting famine.

What Is Famine?

It may be useful to state at the outset what famine is not. Individuals or individual families may be struggling for existence in a state of extreme deprivation and almost continuous undernourishment and malnutrition in most parts of the world, including the industrialized countries. We may even find, amidst affluence, pockets of communities that may be suffering from chronic malnutrition in varying degrees. This is not famine.

Under conditions of war, famine may occur. But famine that is generated by purely political and military upheavals is outside the scope of this study.

Furthermore, it must be pointed out that a very serious confusion of terminology exists. Ordinary hunger is not famine; undernourishment is not famine; malnutrition is not famine, even though all these terms are used interchangeably as if they are synonymous. It is, therefore, important to attempt to clear the confusion.

De Castro and Dumont are two of the most outstanding writers on the problem of the food shortage and the lamentable nutritional condition of the poor in the world at large and, more particularly, in the Third World. Their writings have undoubtedly pricked the consciences of those who suffer from the opposite malaise—that of overnourishment. They have contributed immensely in drawing the attention of the more sensitive and responsive sections of the rich nations. One must especially mention the thrust of their argument, that the chronic shortage of food for the poor of the world is a universal human problem that can be solved if the rich would accept their moral obligation.

This digression was necessitated by an honest desire to pay these outstanding writers their due tribute. But we are presently concerned with the terms they use in their writings.

De Castro, in *The Black Book of Hunger*, states that of the "sixty million deaths recorded annually in the world, thirty to forty million have to be attributed to malnutrition".[1] Rene Dumont, in *The Hungry Future*, refers to the same sixty million annual deaths and attributes "ten to twenty million" to "famine".[2] The difference of about twenty million between the inferences of the two writers indicates a conceptual confusion which abounds in the literature. Other entirely different assessments are not lacking.[3]

De Castro uses such terms as "famine of energy"[4] and "protein famine", while Dumont calls these undernourishment and malnutrition respectively. Dumont defines undernourishment as "nourishment which is inadequate in quality", which is De Castro's "famine of energy", and malnutrition as "nourishment which is defective in quality", which is De Castro's "protein famine". So far so good. But Dumont, basing his assessment on FAO material, states that an average adult requires about 2,700 calories per day. He then explains that undernourishment affects one person in eight, and malnutrition one person in two. "This means, then," he concludes, "that the world is now in the grip of a colossal famine."[5] Quite obviously undernourishment and malnutrition are equated with famine.

Dumont defines famine as "a chronic state of food deficiency which erodes the physical and mental capacities of its victims, ultimately causing premature deaths".[6] This definition seems to coincide with De Castro's "famine of energy" and "protein famine". A "chronic state of food deficiency" is not famine, at least we shall not take it to mean that. A "chronic state of food deficiency" is not in any way different from "nourishment which is inadequate in quantity", and this is undernourishment, or both undernourishment and malnutrition combind.

De Castro tells us that "the Chinese have suffered 1829 famines during the last 2000 years",[7] and Dumont observes, "Between A.D. 1000 and the nineteenth century France was the victim of 150 serious famines—one every six years".[8] If undernourishment and malnutrition were to be equated to famine, these statements would make very little sense, for the former are hardly countable as incidents, and as cases affecting individuals or groups they form continuous phenomena in time and space. Malnutrition and undernourishment are more or less characteristic features of the abject poverty of populations that form the bottom class in any society. They are, therefore, the manifestations of an unfortunate but "normal" condition of existence for the poor in most parts of the world.

Malnutrition is a term that may be properly and specifically limited, as Dumont correctly defines it, to "nourishment which is deficient in quality". Similarly, undernourishment again may be specifically and properly limited to "nourishment which is inadequate in quantity." The question of quality arises when first the question of quantity is settled, and second, when there is a choice. In other words, in a condition of abject poverty and extreme scarcity, it would be idle to talk about deficiency in quality. The satisfaction of food requirements in both quality and quantity is, of course, the ideal; and famine is the very opposite of that ideal. In a famine situation where food for survival is the need, the problem of malnutrition, important as it is in the long run, is secondary.

Any statement that implies a choice between food that is or is not deficient in quantity, and between food that is or is not deficient in quality, is totally outside the context of famine. In adverse circumstances, undernourishment, as a quantitative deficiency of food, is closer to famine than malnutrition, which is a qualitative deficiency of food. In a famine situation, there is simply no choice. The need is for anything that is edible.

Malnutrition and undernourishment, it must be emphasized, relate to poverty and to a more or less "normal" condition of man, so far in *all* countries. That poverty exists, although we must realize its relative character, is as true for Ethiopia as it is for the

USA. In normal circumstances the poor in the USA suffer from *relative* malnutrition and undernourishment just as much as the poor in Ethiopia suffer. A word of caution is in order. It is important to underline the fact that the degree of malnutrition and undernourishment that the poor in Ethiopia suffer is infinitely worse. In other words, the absolute poverty of countries like Ethiopia tends to make malnutrition and undernourishment more general. When Susan George states that, even in the Third World, there are no "hungry countries", but "only poor people living in them", poor people who cannot grow or buy enough food, and then concludes that "there is no fundamental difference" between the developed and underdeveloped countries, she seems to be equating pockets of poverty with pervasive poverty.[9] She presses her point to the extent of saying that if "there were no unemployment benefits in Britain or France, there could perfectly well be honest-to-God famines in both countries affecting over a million peoples.[10] What Susan George would call "honest-to-God famine", poor and starving families, is an always existing and regular phenomenon in the poor countries. This phenomenon is never referred to as famine.

Thus, although differences in the degree to which malnutrition and undernourishment affect the poorest sections of populations may vary from country to country and from time to time, the facts of malnutrition and undernourishment seem so far to be prevalent throughout the world in all countries, including the very rich countries. That is why one must insist on the distinction between malnutrition and undernourishment, or even isolated starvation, on one hand, and famine on the other. The former relates to still unmitigated habitual and common conditions of social malaise, while the latter relates to an unusual and extraordinary manifestation of that same social malaise. It may then be possible to conceive malnutrition and undernourishment not as famine but, perhaps, as latent famine.

In fact Gunnar Myrdal is of the opinion that malnutrition and undernourishment in South East Asia are not limited to the poor. He makes the following statement to prove his point: "Malnutrition and undernourishment do not spare the well-to-do—they are found among the children, women, urban labourers, peasants, clerical workers and other such groups at various economic levels".[11] According to him, there may be societies in the Third World where malnutrition and undernourishment are cultural rather than economic expressions. But, in general, it is perhaps possible to state that

malnutrition and undernourishment in most parts of the world are
indicators of social malaise and economic inequality.

The argument presented here is not that famine is unrelated to
malnutrition and undernourishment; it is rather, that it is not
identical. The argument may be presented differently. All cases of
malnutrition and undernourishment are not necessarily associated
with famine; but all famine is necessarily associated with malnutrition and undernourishment.

Famine is not a mere deficiency of food, but often an absolute
lack of food. For people under famine, the question of the quality
of food simply does not arise. Famine victims have been known to
eat wild roots, the bark of trees, and anything that appears to be
edible, including some poisonous plants and seeds, and even old
cow-hides that have been ground into powder for food. Indeed,
people have sometimes resorted to bestial and barbaric practices. A
husband has eaten his wife, a mother has eaten her babies,[12] and
babies have chewn off their mother's breasts,[13] and free men have
turned themselves into slaves.[14] This is famine.

> In a culture that vocally mourns and openly weeps and shrieks
> at a death, one saw mothers simply covering their dead child's
> face and look at you with blank realization. Perhaps in the
> beginning they cried—with the first child, or a husband or a
> parent. Now it was a loss piled on so many others that had gone
> before, and that had become a way of life.[15]

That is one way of looking at it. Even grief requires energy that
one simply does not have under famine.

Drought is not famine. The confusion between drought and
famine is even more widespread than the confusion between malnutrition, undernourishment and famine. Drought is a meteorological
phenomenon that does not always have a direct relationship with
famine. But it is sometimes flatly stated that the "distinction between drought and famine is not always clear".[16] The confusion
between drought and famine obscures our understanding of the
problem of famine and delays its possible solution. We shall examine the relationship between drought and famine in greater detail
later. For the moment it suffices to state that drought and famine
are not only two entirely different processes, but under certain
conditions they may not even be related to each other.

We may now attempt to define famine more precisely. Famine is the most negative state of food consumption under which people, unable to replace even the energy they lose in basal metabolism, consume whatever is stored in their bodies; that means they literally consume themselves to death. Famine is a general and widespread, prolonged and persistent, extraordinary and insufferable hunger lasting for several months and affecting the majority of the rural population over or more or less extensive area, resulting in total social and economic disorganization and mass death, by starvation. In defining famine, we are not concerned with specific hunger, but with general hunger. The distinction between the two is important to our definition of famine:

> *Hunger* represents that state in an organism in which food would be ingested, if available, either because body nutrients and certain chemicals are depleted or because certain hormones and chemicals are present. *Specific hunger* or appetite reflects the tendency of an animal to ingest certain foodstuffs selectively.[17]

Famine is general hunger affecting large numbers of people in rural areas as a consequence of the non-availability of food for a relatively long time. It is, therefore, a socio-economic crisis with profound consequences for the economic and social fabric of a society.

The problem of food shortage and the danger of famine, and a mechanism for averting the risk was formulated by the Food and Agriculture Organization of the United Nations. As early as December 1951, at its sixth session in Rome, it was resolved:

> 1. That on receiving intimation from a member nation or region that a serious food shortage or famine exists or is likely to develop, which it is unable to cope with from its own resources, the Director-General shall depute one or more Food and Agriculture Organization officials to investigate the nature of the problem with the consent of the government concerned and to report on the extent, if any, of international assistance needed and communicate the report to the United Nations and the interested specialized agencies;
> 2. That when, in the opinion of the Director-General there is an emergency, requiring international relief measures, he shall at his discretion convene forthwith a meeting of the Council or of

interested governments to devise the most practical lines of action
which may be required to bring about prompt, concerted and
effective assistance by governments as well as by voluntary
agencies; and that the Director-General shall thereupon report
the action taken to the Secretary-General of the United Nations
for transmission to the Economic and Social Council.

Subsequently, in January 1952, the General Assembly of the United
Nations in its 365th plenary meeting [Res. 525 (VI)] endorsed the
recommendation of the Economic and Social Council. Member
states of the United Nations are aware of the available opportunity
to avert an impending famine. The World Food Programme is
principally formed for this purpose. Nevertheless, famines not only
continue to occur, but also claim hundreds of thousands of human
lives every now and then.

The response of the ruling class to an impending famine appears
to be remarkably similar everywhere. Officialdom has a characteristic propensity to receive any information on famine with scornful
disbelief. It is possible to substantiate this with numerous cases, but
many of them are so ridiculous that they divert attention from a
serious human tragedy to frivolous tales. The attitude is best mani-
fested by the British official who refused to believe the fact of the
Irish Famine and wrote with an air of authority, "There is such a
tendency to exaggeration and inaccuracy in Irish reports that delay
in acting on them is always desirable."[18] It has already been pointed
out that in Ethiopia, the Ministry of Interior, informed of deaths
by famine, requested for a list of the names of the dead. At another time, when the complaint about some field rats that were
destroying crops reached the Ministry of Interior, the prompt response was: "Send a sample of the rats."[19]

Even when finally famine is accepted as a fact, the scornful disbelief merely turns into an astonishing underestimation of the
magnitude and the intensity of famine. The net result is some perfunctory and ineffectual decision which gets more and more ineffectual as it goes down the bureaucratic ladder.

The victims of such a circumstance, the peasants, endeavour, to
the best of their ability, to survive. They sell whatever is marketable
and eat whatever is edible with a hope that meanwhile some miracle
will take place. How is it that famine always victimizes food producers? We join Pierre Spitz in demanding an explanation for this

apparent paradox:

> The men and women who work on the land, who produce the world's supply of cereals, tubers, oilseeds, vegetables, fruit and meat, hold the lives of all human beings in their hands, including those of the generations to come. In theory, they have the power of life and death. How is it that, during the last ten years, hundreds of thousands of men and women who worked the soil of Asia, Africa and America, who sowed the seeds, harvested the crops and minded the herds have perished for lack of food? How is it that they died of hunger in those parts of the world, whereas most of the people who do not produce foodstuffs were spared?
>
> For, during the same period and in the same countries, no one in ministries, banks or barracks starved to death. Might it not be precisely because agricultural production is of vital importance that those who work on the land in the poor countries are robbed of the power which is theoretically theirs? People who have thus become so powerless that they can no longer be sure of having enough food for themselves, from one year to the next, or even from one season to the next, and who die for that reason, bear witness to the fact that, as the most downtrodden social group, they have lost the most elementary of rights—the right to food, the right to life itself.[20]

The obligation of the peasants to feed others supersedes their right to feed themselves.

Vulnerability to Famine

Vulnerability to famine is a product of a system: a subsistence production system which has three components: the peasant world, the natural forces and the socio-economic and political forces. The peasant world, which includes peasants and nomadic pastoralists, is maintained by two principal sets of relationships. One set of relationship binds the peasant world to natural forces, while another set of relationship ties it to the socio-economic and political forces.

The set of relationships that binds the peasant world to the natural forces is characterized by an almost total dependence of the former on the latter. The dependence of the peasant world on the natural forces yields benefits as well as risks. Under normal conditions, the peasant world's interaction with the natural forces bears some means of subsistence. But when conditions deviate from the expected, the peasant world faces the risk of being without any means of subsistence. The frequency of risk, it may be granted, varies, all other things remaining equal, with the quality of the physical environment. Whether the risks are more than the benefits, or vice versa, for the peasant world, it is not possible to account for the change in terms of the physical conditions. We can only recognize the normal benefits as well as the occasional risks that are involved in the set of relationships between the peasant world and the natural forces. It is important to underline the fact that the benefits derived from this relationship are often normal while the risks are exceptional.

The set of relationship that the peasant world has with the socio-economic and political forces is of an entirely different nature. From this set of relationships the peasant world derives no material benefits. Basically the peasant world is held by a series of obligations which transfer resources in various forms to the socio-economic and political forces. Moreover, this transfer of resources, unlike the risk involved in the peasant world's relationship with the natural forces, is tenaciously persistent and is unmindful of the problems and needs of the peasant world.

It is the occasional risks and the persistent transfer of resources that characterize a subsistence production system. Under certain conditions we can recognize a subsistence production system constituted by the interaction of the peasant world and the natural forces alone. We are, however, presently concerned with a subsistence production system constituted by the peasant world and its relationship of dependence on the natural forces, on one hand, and its relationship of oppression and exploitation by the socio-economic and political force, on the other.

In this context, therefore, the meaning of subsistence production is not limited to what is commonly understood to be production for consumption. In the sense we use it, subsistence production involves risks, oppression and exploitation as well. By subsistence producers we mean rural people, principally peasants and pastoralists, who are exposed to the risks involved in their relationship with the natural conditions and to the oppression and exploitation involved in their relationship with the socio-economic and political forces.

The dependence of agricultural activity on natural phenomena will vary inversely with technological input. Consequently, an agricultural activity that is limited to minimum technological input and that is totally dependent on natural conditions manifests a fundamental weakness of the socio-economic and political super-structure in that society. In the last quarter of the twentieth century it is not possible to rationalize technological ignorance on grounds of isolation or of cost. The fact is that much of agricultural techno-logy is freely available to any government through the United Nations Food and Agricultural Organization and other similar organizations. It is this situation, the inability to use the available agricultural technology, that distinguishes a stagnant agrarian society.

The stagnation of such an agrarian society is systemic; it affects the relationship between the agrarian society and natural conditions as well as the relationship between that society and its socio-econo-mic and political forces. It is the totality of this stagnant condition that we refer to as a subsistence production system.

Subsistence producers lie between the conditions of the physical environment and the socio-economic and political organization of the society, and are affected by both. With the conditions of the physical environment subsistence producers maintain a very delicately balanced relationship and are fully aware of the risks if and when this balance is disturbed. Ignorance may pervade their understanding of the process of nature and may limit their possible action. But certainly they neither claim ignorance nor is it possible to attribute it to them when it comes to the everpresent possibility of sudden and potentially catastrophic change in the normal condi-tions of the physical environment.

Now the question arises: If subsistence producers are fully aware of possible changes in the conditions of the physical environment and of the risks involved, how is it that they are unable to store sufficient supply of food during the good years to last them through the bad years? But we have already stated that subsistence pro-ducers are held with the socio-economic and political organization by another set of relationships, relationships that are characterized by oppression and exploitation. Objectively, there are good years and bad years and, perhaps, more good years than bad ones. Sub-jectively, however, insofar as the peasants are concerned, there are no good years at all. What is objectively a good year is distinguish-ed from a bad one in terms of the relationship between the condi-tions of the physical environment and subsistence producers. This relationship, although unpredictable and full of hardship, is accepted by the subsistence producers as being the best one, in the circumstances, for eking out a living. But from the point of view of subsistence producers, the generally salutary effects of the relationship between them and the conditions of the physical environment are considerably reduced by their relationship with the socio-economic and political forces of the society.

The relationship between subsistence producers and the socio-economic and political forces, unlike the one that binds the former with the physical environment, does not yield even occasional material benefits; it is as unmindful of the precarious life of subsistence producers as it is persistent in its demands. Subsistence producers have no chance of holding reserves of grain or cash, because they are forced to share their produce with many claimants, after which they are left with a food supply that can only last them for six to nine months of the year. That is why we can say there is no good year for subsistence producers.

The claimants are many. The government demands all types of taxes; the church has similar taxes on its land; the landlords want rent; the traditional elders want their dues; government officials require something; usurers want their money plus exorbitant interest; the dead cry for their tribute; and spiritual and social needs impose expensive ceremonies. Subsistence producers have an impressive array of obligations, but hardly any rights. The consequence of living at, or below, subsistence level is, for subsistence producers, to remain outside the market or cash economy. Unmitigated exploitation leading to abject poverty precludes the development of commerce, or what Alfred North Whitehead calls "the growth of persuasive intercourse within the texture of society".[21] Whitehead makes two important points: first, that the "merit of commerce lies in its close relation to technology", and second, that the "novelty of experience promoted by commerce suggests alternatives in ways of production".[22] These are particularly pertinent remarks that contribute immensely to explain the economic stagnation of subsistence producers.

Vulnerability to famine, therefore, is much more a function of the relationship between subsistence producers and the socio-economic and political forces rather than a function of the relationship between the former and the conditions of the physical environment. An agricultural population must first be made vulnerable to famine by the socio-economic and political forces *before* any adverse natural factor initiates the process of food shortage that inevitably leads to famine. But once food shortage, whatever its origin, is recognized as a fact, it is transformed from an adverse effect of physical nature into a social responsibility. In other words, vulnerability to famine which is created by social forces, an act of commission, is exacerbated by the intervening adverse effects of physical nature which, in turn, exposes the failure of the social forces to act, an act of omission, and leads subsistence producers directly into the catastrophe of famine (Figure 1).

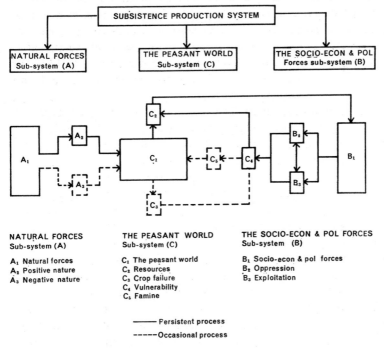

NATURAL FORCES
Sub-system (A)

A₁ Natural forces
A₂ Positive nature
A₃ Negative nature

THE PEASANT WORLD
Sub-system (C)

C₁ The peasant world
C₂ Resources
C₃ Crop failure
C₄ Vulnerability
C₅ Famine

THE SOCIO-ECON & POL FORCES
Sub-system (B)

B₁ Socio-econ & pol forces
B₂ Oppression
B₃ Exploitation

——— Persistent process
----- Occasional process

FIGURE 1

In a nutshell, this is the conceptual framework of this study. We shall now attempt to expound this more concretely and in greater detail.

This study is an attempt to demonstrate convincingly that famine is fundamentally a result of socio-economic disorganization and political irresponsibility. The central idea of this study is that famine is neither the work of God nor that of nature, but of man and his institutions. Rather, it is an inseparable characteristic of a subsistence production system which includes the socio-economic organization, institutions of governmental administration, and the exercise of political power as well as the use and management of available resources. Politically and economically the subsistence producer, whether owner-cultivator, tenant, or nomadic pastoralist, forms the bottom stratum of the society. He is very marginal both in the exercise of his political rights and in his contributions to the market economy on his own behalf. Traditional and governmental institutions as well as the market mechanisms together with rural disorganization conspire against him, and keep him perpetually very near or just below the bare subsistence level. It is this condition that is pregnant with famine.

Government, government officials, traditional patrons, landlords, rich farmers, and merchants created the disorganized, illiterate, weak and voiceless mass of peasants. Insatiable greed has eroded traditional moral values. Without any moral basis and without any sense of accountability to either God or man, and armed with centralized political power as well as the means of enforcing it, the functions of government become personal and create a condition for private law for private interest. Bureaucratic capitalism in its primitive and most ruthless form becomes the instrument of oppression and exploitation, especially of the disorganized and weakest majority of the population, the peasants. In its general form this fact has been recognized by many scholars. Barrington Moore, Jr., writing about what he calls the landed aristocracy, states that, where commercial farming has not developed, "It is likely to try to maintain its style of life in a changing world by extracting a larger surplus out of the peasantry."[23] He expresses it better when he says that the "failure of commercial farming to take hold on any very wide scale made the situation worse, since it meant that there was scarcely any alternative to squeezing the peasant".[24] Maurice Duverger expresses the same idea in a different way:

> The scarcity situation usually causes inequality, with a privileged minority enjoying plenty while the masses suffer serious privation. Frequently, the greater the general poverty, the more ostentatious the oligarchies are. In countries where there is continuous famine, fatness is a sign of power. When the populace wears rags, the privileged wear brocade and gold; when the populace lives in

wretched slums or sleeps in the open air, the wealthy build rich palaces. This situation whereby a small number of people enjoy wealth and luxury in the midst of a starving crowd is of its nature explosive.[5]

The need for ostentation reinforced by advertisements and power turns the peasantry into the most easily exploitable mass. We may, however, note that Moore's idea of "peasant revolution" may not be applicable to Ethiopian reality. Neither does it appear possible to accept James C. Scott's idea of "peasant politics"[26] in the Ethiopian context.

Ethiopian peasants were for quite a long time a depoliticized mass playing only a very marginal role in the incessant conflict for political supremacy. In one way or another the various social institutions have inculcated into their mind a very abstract sense of importance which is based on society's dependence on the peasantry for its food supply. In practice, however, peasants are hardly better off than the almost completely dehumanized and rejected social group, the artisans. It is only obligations that peasants have. The term *ghebbar,* which literally means "one who pays taxes or tribute", became derogatory because it accentuated the various obligations of peasants to government and its officials, to traditional local authorities, to the clergy, and to all those who possessed guns. One Ethiopian proverb states literally: The white poor (man) pays white honey. It means that the most destitute person, turned pale or white by starvation, pays the most highly valued product of his labour as tribute. Another proverb tells us: The living pay tribute to kings and the dead pay theirs to the clergy. In Ethiopia, the dead are a tremendous economic burden on the living, for they exact their own heavy taxes in the form of expensive services of remembrance.

Ethiopian peasants do recognize the claim of others on them, or to use Scott's phrase "the irreducible claims of outsiders",[27] but it cannot be said that they either recognize or claim their own rights. To claim a right that is not given is, in effect, to revolt. It appears that it is necessary to make a distinction between peasant rebellions and rebellions in which peasants participate. A politically ambitious person or a disgruntled official may take refuge in some rural area and, by exploiting the peasants' condition of existence, mobilize them for his purpose. This can hardly be called a peasants' rebellion. It may be said that Ethiopian history is full of such cases.

But genuine peasant rebellion, spontaneous or otherwise, initiated, organized, directed and controlled by the peasants themselves, is a rarity. It seems reasonable, therefore, to insist that a distinction be made between the use of peasant forces for a political purpose that peasants neither know nor understand, and an independent peasant uprising to assert a claim on unrecognized rights.

Scott begins, as he himself states, with R.H. Tawney's metaphor that "the position of the rural population is that of a man standing permanently up to the neck in water, so that even a ripple is sufficient to drown him".[28] This eminently lucid and accurate metaphor, characteristic of Tawney's writings, expresses the existential condition of peasants not only in China but in Ethiopia as well. It is a condition for anything but a rebellion. A "man standing *permanently* up to the neck in water", with his life at the mercy of "a ripple", is hardly in a position to rebel. The socio-economic and political condition in Ethiopia is like Tawney's metaphorical water, which is, as far as the peasants are concerned, a condition of utter helplessness, of vulnerability to famine. We take the ripple as some natural factor that only aggravates the situation.

The Ethiopian peasants living in disorganized, widely scattered hamlets, and permanently preoccupied with attempts to alleviate the nagging daily hunger of themselves and their families as well as the problem of meeting "the irreducible claims of outsiders", have hardly any energy or the means to fight against well-equipped armed forces with deadly modern weapons. No matter how strongly the peasants feel the injustice, the oppression, and the exploitation, as realists they find it better to rely on their commonsense and almost inexhaustible patience than on rebellion, which, even if it materializes, will almost certainly fail to achieve any purpose. So peasants have found it easier to submit individually in view of the absence of a collective will. An old peasant in Chercher (Harerghe) complained about the very high rent of grazing land. It was suggested to him that, if all the peasants in the area cooperated in refusing to pay rent and allowed their livestock to graze on the unfenced fields, there might be a chance that nothing would happen. His prompt reply was: "Yes, it would be possible if all the people here had the same religion and belonged to the same linguistic group, and had a similar stand against oppression. But there is a medley of people here, and we do not trust each other." He delivered what may be considered as a sound lecture on political geography.[29] In a rather different way, this peasant appears to confirm Moore's generalization that a "highly segmented society that depends on diffuse sanctions for its coherence and for extracting the surplus from the underlying peasantry is nearly immune to peasant rebellion because opposition is likely to take the form of creating another segment".[30]

And so the socio-economic and political condition makes sure that the peasants' life will remain permanently precarious, hanging on the slender probability of nature's continuous generosity. When nature fails them, disaster takes a steeper gradient and brings the peasants, especially the poor peasants, to the precipice of famine, in full view of all the socio-economic and political forces of the society.

In an underdeveloped agrarian society the peasant world mainly consists of the peasant himself and his major means of production land and livestock. All the three factors of production of the peasant world—labour, land and livestock—almost totally depend on the forces of nature for their well-being. Conversely, all the three factors may be periodically adversely affected by one, or a combination, of several forces of nature. The spread of an epidemic disease may paralyze labour and decrease or even totally stop production. The spread of livestock or plant diseases may have a similar effect. The land and its capacity to produce may be adversely affected by soil erosion, drought, or frost. The world of the peasant can do very little to withstand effectively such adverse forces of nature. As a consequence, food production may periodically decline considerably, or it may even be totally lost. From nature's side, therefore, this ripple, to continue with Tawney's metaphor, that manifests itself in periodic decline or loss of production in the peasant world and threatens to drown him in famine is but the final act of a long and continuous socio-economic process that culminates in the helpless vulnerability of peasant existence.

The interaction of the peasant world with the government and the socio-economic structure produces the peasant world's vulnerability to famine. The meagre production of the peasant world continuously flows out in form of taxes, rent, debt, bribery, corruption and various forms of extortion. This persistent and insatiable demand for sharing the produce of the peasants manifests at once both the political weakness of peasants and the cause of their abject poverty. It is "the irreducible claims of outsiders" that, by its persistent and insistent demands, depletes the produce of the peasants.

This persistent claim on the produce of the peasants has at least three major effects. First, the peasants are kept permanently at a level of, or below, subsistence, meeting the claims of outsiders before they satisfy their own basic needs. The lot of the peasants is, therefore, one of struggle for existence. Second, the peasants' capacity to save becomes, in such circumstances of marginal living, unthinkable, and because they do not save, they have no potential for raising the productivity of their land through some form of investment. The result is that peasants are forced to remain attached to the traditional methods of production. Third, and most important, the persistent demands of outsiders renders the peasants incapable of commercializing their farms. The fact that most peasants remain outside the market economy, with hardly any commercial transactions, reduces their capacity for the acquisition and retention of cash.

The net result of the consistent flow of the peasants' produce to outsiders is to leave the peasants without any grain reserves in store or any cash in their hands. Ultimately, this is the fact of vulnerability that exposes them to famine. In circumstances that may be considered normal, the peasants manage to survive through the year by tightening their belts and by borrowing money or grain. But when a certain natural factor intervenes to reduce or totally destroy their expected crop, the peasants find themselves unable to feed themselves and their families. At such times the requirements are of such a magnitude that peasants find it impossible to indulge in borrowing money, and lenders become reluctant to take the risk, preferring instead to force peasants to sell their property cheaply. As a consequence, the general reaction of the peasants will be to sell whatever marketable property they have and emigrate en masse. It is clear, therefore, that adverse effects of nature act on the vulnerable condition of the peasants, a condition that is created by the political and socio-economic organization that plunders the peasants incessantly. In the absence of this crucial condition of vulnerability, famine may not occur.

The peasant world is made vulnerable to famine by the subsistence production system. In other words, the peasants' vulnerability to famine is a function of the subsistence production system. The probability that famine will occur periodically in a subsistence production system is high while it is low in a commercialized farming system.

In a subsistence production system which is constituted by peasant farming and pastoralism that is almost totally dependent on the quality of the physical environment and the regularity of the natural phenomena, on one hand, and the process of incessant exploitation of the subsistence producers by the ruling class and the ascending petty bourgeoisie, on the other, famine is almost inevitable. As has been sufficiently demonstrated by Moore, the growing need for cash on the part of the ruling class and the budding petit bourgeoisie will make the commercialization of farming a necessity. Initially, the objective of commercializing farming will be to maximize returns with as little investment as possible by acquiring the best land. Very often this new venture produces one of two consequences: either subsistence producers, peasants and pastoralists are reduced to seasonal agricultural labourers, or they are pushed into marginal land. In either case, the condition of life for peasants and pastoralists is very much aggravated. All other things remaining equal, therefore, those areas where the peasants have been reduced to seasonal agricultural labourers, and where they have been pushed into the less productive and marginal land will be more vulnerable to famine. In other words, the poor quality of the physical environment accentuates the vulnerability to famine created by the continuous exploitation. Since exploitation is taken as the determining factor of vulnerability to famine, the part played by the poor quality of the physical environment remains valid even in areas where peasants and pastoralists are neither reduced to agricultural labourers nor pushed from their original land. Where peasants and pastoralists are not dislocated by imposed commercialization of farming, pressure of population and fragmentation of farms, as well as the impoverishment of the soil, overuse and overgrazing, reduce the quality of the physical environment.

We shall attempt to demonstrate that there is a direct relationship between famine and subsistence production as well as between subsistence production and the quality of the physical environment, on one hand, and famine, on the other. It will also be necessary to show the direct relationship between commercialization of farming and the quality of the physical environment, together with the inverse relationship between these two, on one hand, and famine on the other.

Vulnerability to famine is a deficiency, it must be emphasized, of the sub-system, and not only of the economic activity of subsistence production. One of the components of this vulnerable sub-system is the poor quality of the physical environment, for which partly the peasants and pastoralists themselves and partly the socio-economic organization of the society as a whole are responsible.

The hardship that societies encounter in their attempts to manipulate their physical environment consists in deficiency of certain desirable qualities and in relatively higher demand for inputs. Arid areas, for instance, are generally poor in agricultural resources, and people find it extremely difficult to survive under their restrictive and demanding conditions. Where possibilities exist for irrigated agriculture, the technology and the capital that are required impose severe limitations. Mountain areas may initially provide some opportunities for farming. But unless farming is attended to with special skills of cultivation and soil protection, the high rate of erodibility in mountain areas will gradually result in the impoverishment of the soil, and this may lower or even totally curtail any returns from the land under a traditional method of agricultural production.

Even if we move outside agricultural activity, the peculiar demands of the physical environment are present. Road building in mountainous areas is more laborious and more expensive than in relatively flat areas. The point is that, even for societies that have the technology and the capital, there are special difficulties in coping with the peculiar conditions of the physical environment. For societies that have neither the technology nor the capital, the problems become simply overbearing. Societies that have somehow assured for themselves the satisfaction of their basic needs may view the problem of the physical environment as challenging, and appropriate responses may be generated. But for people who are still struggling for existence and who are physically, mentally, and emotionally tormented daily by the most basic need for food and water, the situation is entirely different. Such societies attempt to respond only to that most pressing and immediate need, and, therefore, have neither the energy nor the inclination to create or to respond to other needs.

And so the availability of agricultural resources such as land, soil, and water, together with the variability of the mean annual rainfall as well as the physical environment's susceptibility to pests and diseases, constitutes the quality of the physical environment. One of the distinguishing characteristics of the subsistence production sub-system is the poor quality of the physical environment. As an economic activity, subsistence production may be defined at its best: production=consumption. But, as many writers like to point out, there is no region or country which has pure or absolute subsistence production. That subsistence production exists in relative terms, however, is hardly debatable. There are many countries in the world, and many regions in various countries, where the level of commercialization or monetization of agriculture is so low that subsistence production is almost readily recognizable. Of course, it is possible even to recognize various levels of subsistence production.

We may identify subsistence production with the following five characteristics: (*i*) small and often fragmented land; (*ii*) primitive tools and implements; (*iii*) production geared to personal needs rather than to market; (*iv*) lack of alternative or seasonal employment opportunities; and (*v*) almost total absence of reserves of either grain or cash.

In the first place most peasants cultivate an area of land that is too small, often less than one hectare. Even this small holding is fragmented into two to four or even more plots. The small holdings are limited by either inheritance or the peasants' capacity which in turn is determined by the available labour and ox-power.

Second, the peasants' methods of production have hardly changed for many centuries. They still depend, for much of the farm work, on their own labour and that of their oxen. The tools and implements they use are poor and inefficient. The use of artificial fertilizer, even if and when they know about it, is beyond their means. Rats, insects and various plant diseases destroy much of their crop. In many parts of the country, loss through poor storage and winnowing is high.

Third, peasants do not generally produce commodities. Their production is geared to their own needs rather than to the market. As a result, peasants rarely make the rational choice of using their land for high-value crops. It can be stated that the concept of economic productivity is quite alien to them. Moreover, there is no specialization of production: each peasant attempts to produce almost all the crops that he needs. Diversification is practised not only as an insurance against risk, but also as a means of self-sufficiency.

Fourth, neither in the rural areas nor in the small towns can peasants find seasonal employment opportunities. A few enterprising peasants may combine farming with some small-scale trading. But the vast majority of peasants have no means of acquiring a cash income to raise their purchasing power or to afford some cash reserves.

The fifth characteristic is really the combined effect of the previous four. Peasants have no reserves of grain or cash. Subsistence production is an activity in which peasants are perennially engaged in the struggle for existence in the most basic sense, that of producing what will keep them alive till the next harvest. Very often they fail to achieve that objective, their produce lasting them for only from six to nine months. The poorer subsistence producers occupy marginal areas. The case of the pastoral nomads, occupying the hotter and drier lowlands, is obvious enough. Even on the highlands, however, poor peasants cultivate land that is not only too small and fragmented, but also rocky and impoverished by overuse and misuse. For the vast majority of peasants, therefore, output is so low that grain reserves are simply out of the question.

Since they do not produce primarily for the market and since they have hardly any surplus that will involve them in any major cash transaction, subsistence producers are marginal to the cash economy. With neither skill nor drive, the cash-earning capacity of the subsistence producers is practically non-existent. And so cash reserves are out of the question. In times of crises, therefore, subsistence producers have neither the grain reserves with which they may frugally alleviate their problem of food shortage, nor the necessary cash reserves with which they may buy food from the market. Their possible reserves in livestock, at times of crisis, fetch such low prices that, even if their beasts were sold, the price could hardly cover food for more than a few days.

If we accept the fact that in, general, subsistence producers are essentially and almost exclusively engaged in producing food for themselves and their families on a harvest-to-harvest basis without any reserves of food or cash to carry them over a critical period, then we have recognized a system that is falsely self-sufficient and unreasonably reliant on the capricious physical conditions of the environment and the exploitative socio-economic organization of the society. It is precisely the false self-sufficiency and the groundless reliance on the physical conditions, and the persistent exploitation, that render subsistence production basically vulnerable to famine.

The major factor that produces vulnerability to famine is government. A famine situation exposes the failure of governments for various reasons. The mere existence of a subsistence system of production with all its weaknesses and vulnerability demonstrates, on the part of governments, a lack of sensitivity to the problems of the rural masses. But we also know that the vulnerable subsistence production activity is not only tolerated, but even exploited, thus aggravating its food problems. Moreover, when crop failure occurs in vulnerable regions, famine very often is allowed to take its natural course without any government intervention, until it is too late. The frequency of famine in a given country, therefore, is at once the expression and the fault of economic institutions. In a normal year, the produce of the peasants is shared by official and traditional authorities. This means that peasants' consumption as well as their capacity to keep some reserves is drastically curtailed. Exploitation condemns the peasants to a permanently precarious living, the basis of their vulnerability. The following verse expresses the resentment of peasants and their perception of their own lives, which are compared to that of the monkeys':

If land tax we must pay,
So must the monkey,
For is it not the same land,
That it scratches with its hand?[31]

Imperialism, mainly operating through cultural aggression, augments and strengthens the parasitic character of the ruling class and the elite in order to make it a better and more amenable host for its own parasitic intentions. By merely manipulating the form of traditional authority and giving it sufficient political and military support, it revitalizes an otherwise dead system of rule. Whether the oligarchy is composed of traditionalists or modernists matters little, as long as it can play a formally legitimate role and accommodate imperialism in exchange for political and military support.

Dependence on imperialism is ascertained through new consumption habits as well as through the instigation of potential enemies, thereby creating new demands for armament. As these habits and demands increase, the exploitation of the masses becomes more and more brutal, for it is by reducing the satisfaction of their basic needs that they maintain the insatiable bureaucratic capitalists. Consequently, the poorer the country the greater becomes the need for exploitation by government and the more severe the exploitation. For the rural masses, this means greater vulnerability to famine. We shall attempt to demonstrate the validity of this argument in the following pages. We shall first highlight the problem of famine in Ethiopia with a brief account of the historical background, followed by reviews of four famines in Ethiopia.

NOTES

[1]Jose De Castro, *The Black Book of Hunger*, (Beacon Press, Boston, 1969), p. 13.

[2]Rene Dumont, *The Hungry Future*, (London, 1970), p. 35.

[3]See Paul R. Ehrlich, Anne H. Ehrlich, John P. Holden, *Ecoscience: Population, Resources, Environment*, (San Francisco, 1977), p. 291.

[4]*The Black Book of Hunger, op. cit.*

[5]*The Hungry Future, op. cit.*, pp. 33-34.

[6]*Ibid.*, p. 33.

[7]Jose De Castro, *The Geography of Hunger*, (London, 1955), p. 33.

[8]*Op. cit.*, p. 23.

[9]Susan George, *How the Other Half Dies: The Real Reason for World Hunger*, (Montclair, 1977), p. 10.

[10]*Loc. cit.*

[11]Gunnar Myrdal, *The Asian Drama: An Inquiry into the Poverty of Nations*, (Penguin Book, Clinton, 1968), Vol. I, p. 549.

[12]See Richard Pankhurst, *The Great Ethiopian Famine of 1888-1892*, Mimeographed copy (HSIU, Addis Ababa, 1964), pp. 30-34.

[13]The writer had the misfortune of witnessing this in Tigray in 1959.

[14]Richard Pankhurst, *The Great Ethiopian Famine, op. cit.*, p. 33.

[15]Liam Nolan, *The Forgotten Famine*, (A Mercier Book, Dublin, 1974), p. 9.

[16]See, for instance, *Proceedings of the Symposium on Drought in Botswana*, (The University Press of New England, Hanover, New Hampshire, 1978), p. 41, also pp. 137-138. See also Benjamin Goodwin Wisner Jr., *The Human Ecology of Drought in Eastern Kenya*, (Ph. D. dissertation, Clark University, Worcester, 1977), p. 68.

[17]Saul Balagura, *Hunger: A Biosychological Analysis*, (New York, 1973), p. vii. See also, p. 133.

[18]Cacil Woodham-Smith, *The Great Hunger: Ireland 1845-49*, (A Four Square Book, London, 1965), p. 35.

[19]Ethiopia, Ministry of Agriculture to Ministry of Interior, 21/1/57, and Ministry of Interior to Wellega, 4/2/57.

[20]Pierre Spitz, "Silent Violence: Famine and Inequality", *Rev. Int. Sc. Soc.*, Vol. XXX (1978), No. 4, p. 867.

[21]Alfred North Whitehead, *Adventure of Ideas*, (A Mentor Book, New York, 1955), p. 90.

[22]*Ibid.*, p. 91.

[23]Barrington Moore, Jr., *Social Origins of Dictatorship and Democracy: Lord and Peasant in the Making of the Modern World*, (Boston, 1966), p. 460.

[24]*Ibid.*, p. 472.

[25]Maurice Duverger, trans. Robert North and Ruth Murphy, *The Idea of Politics: The Uses of Power in Society*, (London, 1966), p. 63.

[26]James C. Scott, *The Moral Economy of the Peasant: Rebellion and Subsistence in Southeast Asia*, (London, 1978).

[27]*Ibid.*, p. 2.

[28]*Ibid.*, p. 1.

[29]Verbal communication.

[30]Barrington Moore Jr., *op. cit.*, p. 459.

[31]My own translation from Amharic.

PART II

THE PROBLEM OF FAMINE

Chapter Two

The Problem of Famine in Ethiopia

Historical Background

· Although this is not a study of the history of famine in Ethiopia, it may be appropriate to set the stage with a brief historical sketch. The history of famine in Ethiopia goes back for centuries. Although a systematic study is still lacking, we are grateful to Richard Pankhurst for his articles which give a bird's eye-view of the history of this pernicious problem: "The Great Ethiopian Famine of 1888-1892".[1] "The History of Famine and Pestilence in Ethiopia Prior to the Founding of Gonder",[2] and "The Earliest History of Famine and Pestilence in Ethiopia: A Note on the Egyptian Deaths".[3] Using Ethiopian documentary sources as well as foreign travellers' accounts, Richard Pankhurst, in these three articles, traces the history of famine in Ethiopia from about the ninth to the seventeenth centuries plus the last part of the nineteenth century. More accurately, Pankhurst's studies begin in about 1252 and stop at about 1635, with nothing between 1635 and 1888. Moreover, no attempt has been made to differentiate between famine and epidemic diseases.

Nevertheless, Pankhurst's articles are quite sufficient to serve our purpose of presenting a brief background of the history of famine in Ethiopia. It seems that, between 1250 and 1280, there were some seven famine years: 1252, 1258-1259, 1272-1273, 1274-1275.[4] In the fourteenth century, according to Pankhurst, there was one "cruel famine" and an "unidentified epidemic", the first in the first half and the latter in the second half of the century.[5] In the fifteenth century there were again two epidemics, one in 1435-1436 and another "some time between the years 1454 and 1468".[6] The following century witnessed at least four famines, around 1520, 1543-1544, 1559, and another in 1567-1568.[7] Finally, between 1610 and 1636, there were some eight famine years, in 1611, 1618-1619, 1625, 1627 and 1633-1635.[8]

There seems to be some problem in dating the famines. For instance, in his earliest article on famine, Pankhurst states, "No less than eleven major famines occurred in the two centuries from 1540 to 1752, namely in 1540, 1543, 1623, 1650, 1653, 1678, 1700, 1702, 1747, 1748 and 1752."[9] We may, however, get a more complete picture of the history of famine in the near future. Such a history must include not only the dates and the presumed causes, but also the intensity and the extent of famine in a systematic way.

We shall now consider four famines in greater detail: The famine of 1888, The Tigray Famine of 1958, The Wag-Lasta Famine of 1966 and The Wello Famine of 1973.

The Ethiopian Famine of 1888-1892

The Famine of 1888 serves to demonstrate two points. The first is that one of the three factors of production in a subsistence system, in this case oxen, can, if adversely affected, bring about the collapse of the whole production system. The second point is the total helplessness of both government and people, in face of this disastrous situation and the unhampered spread of the disease to all parts of the country, and beyond, into East Africa.

In November 1887, the Italians brought some 800 horses and 1000 mules to Massawa.[10] These animals, as it was learnt later, brought the rinderpest disease with them. This is one version of the story. Another version is that Ras Alula's soldiers took some cattle as spoils which, presumably, were infected with rinderpest.[11] Whichever way the disease might have been introduced onto the highlands of Ethiopia, by February 1888, about four months after the animals landed in Massawa, three-quarters of the cattle in the territory of Bahir Negash (now Eritrea) had died of rinderpest. Four months later, in June 1888, the plague was spreading its disaster in Tigray.

Once the plague reached the Tigrean Plateau it could easily spread southwards with remarkable regularity. Where the density of cattle population was higher, and where mobility and contact was relatively easier, the plague could spread much faster. By February 1889, the cattle in Bahir Negash, Tigray, Beghemdir, Wello, Gojjam, and Shewa had almost been wiped out. At the beginning of 1890 the rinderpest had already reached Italian Somaliland. By 1892 the plague had killed about 90% of the Ethiopian cattle population. (See Figure 2.)

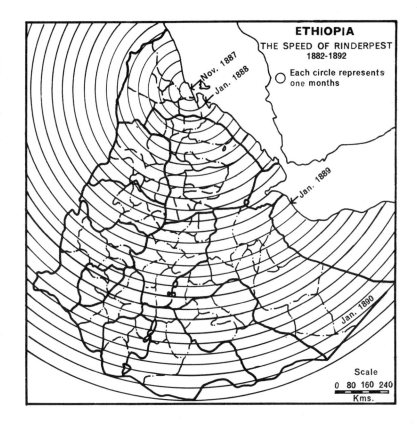

FIGURE 2

Without their cattle, especially oxen, Eihiopian peasants could not carry on their normal farm operations. One of the major pillars of the Ethiopian subsistence production was almost totally destroyed by the plague. Peasants reverted to an even more primitive method of

farming, that of putting human beings under the yoke to plough
the field. Emperor Minilik himself set the example of ploughing
with the hoe or pickaxe. But this effort was not sufficient to prevent
food shortage in all parts of the country. As a result, famine grip-
ped the whole country. Nobody knows for sure how many persons
died. But some people estimated, perhaps with some exaggeration,
that about one-third of the population of the country had died of
famine between 1888 and 1892. But a description of the famine, a
description which Richard Pankhurst thinks is "one of the most
terrible ever penned", is worth quoting in full:

> Here and there, were abandoned corpses, their faces covered with
> rags; one, horrible to see, appeared to move, so swarming was it
> with insects which crept over the decomposing limbs in the burn-
> ing sun. The dead awaited the hyenas, the living awaited death.
> From a thicket issued a thin murmur of voices, while hands
> devoid of flesh stretched forth quaking with the last shiver of
> life. Here in the sand a dying man with his last energy raises him-
> self on his back, glares with staring glassy and unseeing eyes,
> gives out a rattle and drops to the ground, striking his neck and
> back as he falls, there a crouching woman who can no longer
> speak rocks with continuous motion a child of four or five years
> near to exhaustion and devoting herself to her pallid dear one
> mutters *meskin, meskin* (cries for alms) in a faint, hoarse voice.
> We are accosted for help, and from their death beds suddenly
> rises a mob of skeletons whose bones can be seen under the taut
> skin as in the mummified skeleton of Saint Bernard. They try to
> follow us, they also crying out *meskin, meskin*; exhausted, they
> fall down, attempt to rise, stumble, fall again and trail behind
> us on all fours, calling for help with groans and shrieks. Mothers
> exhaustedly heave their sucklings from the ground and follow us
> weeping and moaning, and pointing for us at their shrivelled
> breasts. We distribute some *lire*, a form of succour laughable in
> such indigence, useless to those who will be dead in an hour . . .
> I flee to escape from it and stumble on a young boy scratching in
> the excrement of camels to find a grain of *durra*; horrified I turn
> away only to see other boys whom the *zapte* (native police) are
> driving away by force from the carcass of a horse the stinking
> leftover of the hyenas, from this carcass they snatch—biting with
> their teeth at its entrails, the entrails because they are softer,

softer because they are one most putrid. I flee horrified, stupified, shamed by my impotence, hiding my watch chain in shame, ashamed in my self of the breakfast which I had eaten, of the dinner which awaited me . . .[12]

Rinderpest, as a natural factor introduced to the country by man, could proceed without let or hindrance not only to cover the whole country but even to spill over its borders, into Somalia and eastern Africa. The society was helpless and could not arrest the progress of this terrible plague, which took about four years to cover the whole country and to take a heavy toll of the cattle. Since vaccination against rinderpest was unknown at that time, the society's helplessness in the face of the plague may be understandable. But that no attempt was even made to control the movements of livestock may be taken as the inaction and failure of the society to organize itself in such a way as to reduce the devastating effect of rinderpest that made famine inevitable.

The Tigray Famine of 1958

A very devastating famine that the population of Addis Ababa knew hardly anything about is the famine in Tigray, in 1958. By the summer of 1958 the crisis was already two years old.[13] People had started dying. A letter from the Governor-General of Tigray to the Ministry of Interior asks: "How can we passively watch when human beings, created in the image of God, are thrashed to death by starvation?"[14] Large numbers of people were dying and still larger numbers were emigrating to the surrounding areas.

The famine in Tigray was a subject under such a taboo in Addis Ababa that it was only in February 1954 that the Red Cross wrote a very belated letter, asking for information of the famine in Tigray and Eritrea, to the Ministry of Interior, after thousands of persons had already died.[15] On the very same day, unusually efficiently, the Ministry of Interior informed the Red Cross that the famine-affected population was estimated to be about 1,000,000.[16] Meanwhile, reports of deaths were reaching the Ministry of Interior from various *awrajas* (administrative areas) in Tigray. It was only at this time, in September of 1959, more than two years later, when the famine had sufficiently intensified to claim many lives, that the government began to disclose the news and asked for contributions.

Money for Tigray was collected in various parts of the country, but with hardly any coordination. As a result most of the funds never reached Tigray. In August 1959, Gamo Gofa, not knowing what to do with the 1635 Birr collected for Tigray, asked the Ministry of Interior if the money could be used for repairing churches.[17] A month later the Ministry sharply replied in the negative, without telling them what to do with the money.[18] Jarra *Awraja* informed the Ministry that it had collected 2020.60 Birr for Tigray,[19] but got no instruction on what to do with it. Similarly, a religious association at St. George's Cathedral in Addis Ababa had collected 700.00 Birr.[20] Then the Department of Public Security informed the Ministry of Interior that, out of the 19,864.77 Birr collected for Tigray, it had spent 3,028.75 Birr, and that the balance was available.[21] In August 1961, Shewa authorized Kembata *Awraja* that, since "the crisis is over", to use the 6434.80 Birr collected for Tigray for purchasing a typewriter for Shewa and the remainder for building a clinic in the *Awraja*.[22]

Finally, thirty-two months after the reports of famine deaths reached the Ministry of Interior,[23] the Prime Minister informed the Ministry of Interior that the first substantial relief grain from the United States would soon arrive: 22,000 tons for Eritrea and 10,000 tons for Tigray.[24] Eritrea did not suffer half as much as Tigray. However, in August-September of 1961, only a total of 7,496,413 kg, or about 7.5 tons of wheat and sorghum that came from the United States, was distributed in Tigray.[25]

By the time this shipment of grains had arrived, at the very least 100,000 persons had died, and perhaps many more.[26] Thousands of persons, mostly able-bodied men, had emigrated to other parts of the country.

The causes this disaster varied from time to time, and from place to place. At the beginning, drought was taken to be the cause of the crop failure.[27] Then it was epidemics of mainly small-pox and typhus, but also measles and malaria.[28] Locust invasion was next.[29] In Adwa the crop was damaged by locusts as well as by hailstones.[30] It was reported that Tembien had the same problem of locusts and hailstones.[31] Perhaps it is true that disasters never come alone.

Tigray had hardly recovered from this devastating famine when it entered into another one in 1965-1967, and again one in 1973, from which it has still to emerge.

The Wag-Lasta (Wello) Famine of 1966

Like the severe Tigray Famine of 1958, the Wag-Lasta Famine of 1966, remained unknown to most Ethiopians, let alone to the outside world. Although famine was devastatingly severe in Wag and Lasta in 1966, many *awrajas* in various other parts of the country had also fallen under famine. In many ways the famine of 1966 can be considered as the forerunner to the major famine that has now come to be known as the Wello Famine of 1974.

According to the documents, the first information on the impending Wag-Lasta Famine of 1966 reached the Ministry of Interior through the police, in October 1965.[32] The Ministry of Agriculture, presumably informed by the Ministry of Interior, replied that they were ready to offer "advice and technical assistance".[33] The Ministry of Interior then wrote to Wello, quoting the police report, and requesting a clarification of the situation.[34] More than three months later, in February 1966, the Deputy Governor of Wello informed the Ministry of Interior of the seriousness of the problem and of the fact that large numbers of people were leaving their villages in search of work and food.[35] In May 1966, the Ministry of Interior requested an up-to-date report of the situation.[36] A month later Wello informed the Ministry that there were people starving, and that the situation was very critical.[37]

By August and September 1966, the situation in Wag and Lasta had deteriorated sharply. Reports of severe starvation and of deaths were reaching the Ministry of Interior from other parts of Wello, too. The famine belt was expanding. Dese *Awraja* wrote to the Governor-General of Wello of severe starvation affecting about 60% of the population of the *awraja*.[38] Getting the information that 2730 persons had died of famine in one *mikitil wereda* (sub-district) in Ambassel, the terse response of the Ministry was to request a list of names of the dead![39]

The first reference to indicate that the information on the condition in Wello had reached the Emperor is a letter from the Ministry of Pen to the Ministry of Finance in September 1966.[40] According to this letter, the Emperor had ordered the Ministry of Finance to make a sum of 220,000 Birr available to Wello. Only a few days earlier, the Crown Prince, who was the Governor-General of Wello, had donated 1000 Birr to the famine victims that had gathered in Dese.[41] It is important to note that a decision to do something was made almost one year after the information reached the Ministry of Interior. People had already started dying in many parts of Wello, especially in Wag, Lasta and Ambassel. The question of whether or not 220,000 Birr was adequate is too obvious to merit any further discussion. But how even that decision could not be implemented efficiently and effectively is important.

During and after September 1966, the major topic of the correspondence between Addis Ababa and Dese was the problem of transport. After more than twelve months, some grain finally did reach Dese. But for the starving people of Wello it was still not available. Star Transport Company complained to the Grain Board that they were unable to unload the grain for a whole month.[42] On its part, Wello complained that the truck drivers refused to take the grain to the various *awraja* centres.[43] Wello was also requesting funds for the purchase of mules and donkeys as well as Mercedes trucks.[44] Finally, Wello managed to buy Mercedes trucks, although one of them was eventually carried away with its load of relief grain in the Tirrari river.[45]

While Addis Ababa and Dese were exchanging letters on how to send the grain to the various *awrajas* and on the share of each *awraja*, famine was intensifying and reports of death were increasing. One hundred and thirty-four persons with their babies had walked from Lasta to Addis Ababa to present a petition to the government. The Ministry of Interior paid for their transport and sent them back.[46] In April 1967, the people of Wag *Awraja* presented a petition to their parliamentary representatives, stating that 800 persons had died of famine and epidemic diseases.[47] In July 1967, the Lasta police reported to their head office in Dese, "Since June the number of corpses that are lying unburied all over the place along the roads is great." The police report concluded that unless something is done soon, "There should be no doubt that the region would turn into an uninhabited desert."[48] Similarly, the police in Wag reported that between June and August, 1200 persons had died of famine.[49] In September 1967, Wag *Awraja* informed Wello, with a copy to the Ministry of Interior, that 308 persons had died in one district (anticipating the Ministry's response, a list of their names was included) and that 238 persons had left their villages.[50]

At this time of suffering and death, official bureaucracy was not only content with its leisurely exchange of letters, but was also conducting its normal routine of tax collection and extortion as if nothing was happening. A delegation from Lasta *Awraja* presented their petition on behalf of the population of that *Awraja* to the Ministry of Interior. The petition states that officials were harassing them to pay taxes and tithes, as well as contributions for construction of roads.[51] There is no record to show that the issue was resolved in favour of the petitioners.

It seems clear that government officials believed that the rural population had cash enough for taxes and contributions as well as for purchasing food grains. This is presumably the reason why they sent 10,000 quintals of wheat to Wag and Lasta and some 6000 quintals to be divided between the other *awrajas* to be sold at a reduced price of 18 Birr per quintal. This is an example that invalidates the argument that famine is a problem of distribution of food as a commodity and of soaring food prices at a time of scarcity.

We shall consider only Lasta and Wag, where 10,000 quintals of wheat was available in June 1968 at an even lower price than that fixed earlier.[52] After five months, only 781 quintals out of the 10,000 were sold at a price of 15 Birr per quintal.[53] Within a period of about fourteen months, 472 quintals more, making a total of 1253 quintals, were sold.[54] The remaining 8747 quintals of wheat, like the grain that was sent to be sold in Borena-Sayint (239 quintals), Yejju (300 quintals),[55] and other *awrajas*, was rotting, while storage rent was rising and the poor were dying. In fact, elders of Wag sent a telegram to the Governor of Wello, stating that while "people were dying of starvation, rodents were eating the wheat".[56] Finally, after months of exchange of letters between Wag, Wello, and Addis Ababa, the Council of Ministers decided to authorize the Grain Board to resolve the issue of the rotting grain.[57] But it was not until eight months later that the Grain Board resolved the issue.[58] That it paid 3690 Birr for storage rent in cash for the rotten grain is documented. But that it sold the grain that was by then unfit for human consumption, at a ridiculously low price, to merchants and bakers is not documented.[59]

On the part of the starving and dying, not in any one of the *awrajas* where grain was rotting in storage, is there a record of an attempt to loot. They simply died as lawful citizens, waiting for relief aid. This amazing restraint under hardship, that is noted here only in passing, is characteristic of Ethiopian peasants.

The Wello Famine of 1973

Very much, perhaps too much, has been written on the Wello Famine of 1973 by various people for various reasons.[60] The most thorough study of the Wello Famine of 1973, however, is that made by the Commission of Inquiry.[61] Unfortunately, this study has never been published even in Amharic, although mimeographed copies have been distributed to all government organizations and institutions. It is a meticulously documented and authoritative study on the subject. One hopes that the outside world will some day have the opportunity to read this important work, which still remains untranslated. Most of the material that follows relies on that source.

It was in July 1971 that the people of Awsa *Awraja* petitioned the Governor for food aid. In August of the same year the Governor informed his superiors in Dese, specifying that 13,625 quintals of grain was needed. In September, Dese wrote to the Ministry of Interior in Addis Ababa. Then numerous letters were exchanged not only between Awsa and Dese and the Ministry of Interior, but also between various Ministries and the Council of Ministers. Nothing that matched the gravity and magnitude of the problem was done for almost two years.

In September 1972 the *Awraja* Governor of Rayya and Qobbo wrote to Dese and informed them that drought had hit the *awraja* so hard that grain for food and seed was urgently needed. Moreover, in February 1972 the branch office of the Ministry of Agriculture in Dese wrote to the Ministry of Agriculture, informed them that 97% of the harvest had been destroyed by drought, and requested 400 quintals of grain on credit for seed. The Ministry of Agriculture, in its reply, demanded what guarantee it would have to get its money back from the peasants. In April 1972, Dese wrote to the Ministry of Community Development and received a reply in June. The reply stated that the information was very much exaggerated and lacked precision and that it must, therefore, be more thoroughly studied. Again nothing to match the problem was done.

It was as early as October 1972 that the *Awraja* Governor of Ambassel informed Dese that drought had brought crop failure and that the people were in distress. After this single letter no correspondence on the problem of Ambassel is traceable until twenty-one months later. But in that first letter it was stated that, in the lowland areas, people had already started eating leaves and wild berries.

As already discussed earlier Lasta *Awraja*, together with Wag *Awraja*, was hard hit by the famine of 1966-1968. Although famine had never ceased in the whole *awraja* after 1968, the parliamentary representative of that *awraja*, in a letter written in November 1972, enumerated the *weredas* that suffered from crop failure and requested not aid but a waiver of tithe and taxes. Correspondence on the problem of food shortage and taxes continued almost through 1973. And Wag *Awraja* had been corresponding with Dese since March 1972, although this *awraja*, too, never really recovered from the earlier famine years.

The first information on crop failure from the *weredas* to reach Werre Himeno *Awraja* was in November 1973. But by that time many people were leaving their villages. The first action that Dese took was to telegram the *Awraja* Governor, in January 1974, instructing him to stop the people from leaving their villages.

For Werre Ilu *Awraja* information on famine was rather late, coming in March 1973.

The first report from the *weredas* on drought, acute food shortage and death of livestock reached Yejju *Awraja* in October 1972. The *awraja*, in turn, informed the Dese office in December 1972. Correspondence continued between Yejju and Dese until September 1973, when the people petitioned Dese not only for food aid but also for waiving of taxes. Practically nothing was done until the middle of 1974.

Similarly, written information on the famine of 1973 appears rather late for the relatively more accessible *awrajas* of Dese and Qallu. Dese *Awraja* did not report famine until June 1973. Qallu *Awraja*, too, reported famine at about the same time, although one *wereda* had reported famine one year earlier. But the *awraja* was more efficient in sending an order, in August 1973, to all the *weredas* to remove all carcasses from the roadsides and bury them.

Information on famine from Borena-Sayint and Wadla-Delanta *Awrajas* seems to have taken a strange turn. The earliest information on famine in these two *awrajas* came from the investigating team of the Governor-General of Wello (*see* Table II p. 50). A report from Borena-Sayint *Awraja* did not appear until June 1975. By that time large numbers of people had left the *awraja* and those remaining were under a condition of extreme hardship. Even at that time they were pleading for a waiver of taxes.

For Wadla-Delanta *Awraja* famine became a topic of correspondence after February 1973, in connection with the Wello famine victims who had arrived in Addis Ababa at that time. An order had been sent in January 1974, to all the *weredas* to prevent people from leaving their villages. In March 1974 some *weredas* informed the *awraja* that unspecified worms and drought had devastated crops and that people were in an extremely bad condition. A month later the *awraja* replied by reminding them to pray. By May 1974, no grain had yet reached Wadla-Delanta.

There is sufficient evidence, therefore, to show that there was certainly no lack of information. Government officials at all levels have had information on the imminent famine at least six months in advance, and in many cases more than a year in advance. Even as late as February and March 1973, the government officials found it difficult to believe that large numbers of people in Ethiopia, especially in Wello, were on the verge of mass death. How this catastrophe was exposed is a story that is not widely known.

Early in 1973, when famine was only a coffee-time topic of conversation, the Emperor and his government, the University and the Parliament had more or less definite information on the famine in Wello. As a result some undercurrents of interaction were taking place. We shall attempt to summarize these in the following pages.

The Emperor

One of the most significant events related to the so-called Wello Famine was the Emperor's visit to Wello in November 1972. Two things make this event significant: first, the Emperor returned from Wello without realizing the extremely ripe famine situation in Wello. The people of Wello were not allowed to present a petition to the Emperor. Even the letter written to him by the parliamentarians from Wello prior to his departure apparently never reached him.[62] The Emperor was efficiently and effectively protected from any displeasure that might result from the realization of so serious a problem as famine.[63]

Second, the Emperor's proclamation in Wello illustrates that he was never made to understand the gravity of the problem. This proclamation waived the payment of land, education and health taxes as well as tithe for the period Eth. C. 1942 to 1959 (1950-1967). But the taxes for the period Eth. C. 1960-1964 (1968-1972) were to be spread over the next five years and paid together with the taxes of each year.[64] This presumably charitable act meant that the peasants of Wello were to pay double the amount of taxes from 1973 to 1977, which, as subsequent events showed, was the most terrible famine period.

The Emperor visited Wello again in November 1973. Jack Shepherd states that not "until November, when Haile Selassie went to Wello Province and proclaimed shock at what he saw, was the famine allowed to become public, and the relief foods started coming in".[65] By November 1973, as Jack Shepherd should have known, nearly the whole world had heard about the famine for at least six months. Neither is there any expression of shock in the Emperor's second proclamation in Wello. This proclamation, in effect, partially revoked the one made in November 1972 and waived all taxes for 1960 to 1973 for parts of nine *awrajas* only.[66] Presumably, it was believed that only some pockets of these *awrajas* were in distress. For reasons that are not clear, the *awrajas* of Dese, Qallu and Werre Ilu were excluded from this exemption of taxes. Here again we see that, even in November 1973, the Emperor was far from realizing both the extent and the intensity of famine in Wello. This is in spite of the fact that at least six months earlier he had presided over a meeting during which the Minister of the Interior is supposed to have reported his eyewitness account of the famine in Wello. The rather sharp difference between the written and verbal reports of the Minister quite clearly indicated that the Emperor was protected from the knowledge of the magnitude and the intensity of the famine in Wello.[67] In fact the Minister's report is dated nine days after the meeting.[68]

The University

In January and February 1973, there was a persistent rumour in Addis Ababa that large numbers of people from Wello, in an attempt to escape death by famine, were moving to the south-western and southern provinces in search of work in the coffee-producing areas. Upon hearing that such a group was halted by police in the outskirts of Addis Ababa, on the Asmera road, two members of the University, Abraham Demoz of the Department of Ethiopian Languages and Mesfin Wolde-Mariam of the Department of Geography, went to the scene and saw armed policemen guarding some 60 to 70 tired, hungry and sick people, including women and children, who had walked for weeks from Wello. They were told that some had died on the way. The two faculty members were informed by these hungry people that they were kept in the woods, away from the main road, for six days, and that they were only allowed to come to the roadside after much pleading with the policemen. Since they came to the highway many people had seen them and either brought them food or gave them money. Although the police did not prevent the two faculty members of the University from talking with the people, they did, however, take the licence plate number of their car.

This incident was the origin of the University's involvement with the Wello Famine of 1973. The eye-witness accounts of the two faculty members provided the first reliable information on the famine in Wello. This information was immediately transmitted to high government officials. As a result of this contact, the issue was taken up by the Council of Ministers a few days later. But the view prevailed that this was only the "fabrication" of "rumour-mongers" who thought of nothing but "mischief" and "slander", and prevented timely action.

The government's decision was to falsify "the rumour." On 8 Yekatit 1965 E.C. (15 February 1973) a high-ranking government official appeared on television and, after reminding his listeners that "Ethiopians have a right to movement," and that movements from rural areas are quite "normal", he stated that "the exaggerated rumour seems to arise out of light-heartedness rather than seriousness."[69] The confusion is not limited to what is light-hearted and to what is serious. The official continued his unbelievable explanation that "the reason given by the people was drought and this is now prevalent everywhere. It is, however, the obligation of the people to inform higher authorities whenever there is drought. Since this was not done by the people it appeared that they were not aware of their obligations."[70] This needs hardly any comment. With those preliminary remarks the high official authoritatively stated that the problem was not "serious" for that year (1973) and that "according to experts there is surplus food production and that, therefore, let alone requesting international assistance, we have not even determined how much local assistance from the government is required",[71] if at all necessary.

This television interview, given by a high government official, introduced some doubt on the information gathered from the people who had come from Wello and who were being held on the outskirts to Addis Ababa. It was imperative, therefore, to gather more information on the issue and determine whether the official version or the accounts of the people were correct. It was quite evident that the two accounts sharply contradicted each other, and both could not be true. Apparently, as we shall soon see, the government itself had given the rumour of famine the benefit of the doubt, for it sent a fact-finding team to Wello.

During this search for the truth about the conditions in Wello, contact was established between the two faculty members of the University and some Parliamentary representatives from Wello. It was discovered, not unexpectedly, that the Parliamentarians were extremely indignant about the statements made on television. The representatives from Wello were prepared to take the risk of challenging the government. But subsequent events clearly demonstrated that Parliament, being under the effective control of the government, could not be an effective instrument for exposing the famine, if there was famine.

It was deeply felt by many people in the University that the matter was very urgent and needed immediate action in the form of field investigation. The problem of financing the field investigation was solved when Getachew Haile (Department of Ethiopian Languages) managed to get some funds from the World Council of Churches, and with these a Cessna aeroplane was chartered for a team that was made up of Abraham Demoz, Getachew Haile and Alula Abate (Department of Geography). Abraham had a tape-recorder with him, while Getachew and Alula carried cameras and films.

The team left Addis Ababa on the morning of 6 Miazia (14 April) and returned the next day, in the afternoon of 7 Miazia. There were two days to plan what to do with the numerous photographs and recorded interviews that were brought back. It was decided to use geography as a medium for exposing the terrible truth of the Wello Famine. The photographs were printed in large numbers, and some were enlarged. The walls of the University's Geography Room were covered with these photographs, showing the emaciated bodies of starving people, especially women and children. It must be mentioned, in this connection, that it was the office of the Ethiopian Orthodox Church which provided the team with a Landrover and fuel and enabled it to visit the roadside conditions from Dese to Weldeya in a short time.

On the afternoon of 9 Miazia (17 April) an exhibition camou-
flaged as *Geography and Drought*, was opened in the Department of
Geography of the Faculty of Arts. Apart from the photographs
that were displayed, the recorded interviews were continuously
played on a tape, and a mimeographed four-page report of the
team was distributed. Several hundred students visited this dismal
exhibition. In the evening, the regular students closed all the exits
from the Faculty of Arts Building and invited the evening students
to visit the exhibition.

The next day students gathered in the University Campus and
were preparing to demonstrate against the government's attempts
to conceal the famine. The police entered the campus, clubbed the
students and dispersed them.

But the exhibition of *Geography and Drought* continued not only
in the Geography Room (where the photographs were "stolen," to
be replaced by new prints immediately), but also by illustrated talks
to various missionary and other groups. The cat was finally out of
the bag. It was understood that many of the "stolen" photographs
were sent outside the country, especially to Ethiopian students'
organizations, who passed them on to journalists.

The dissemination of the information on famine was immediately
followed by a fund-raising campaign within the University. This
was a very difficult task indeed. The University students decided to
transfer the money value of their breakfast for 57 days. That was
the largest single contribution. Willing members of the rest of
the University community contributed 5% of their monthly salary,
some for two months, and the University administration cooperated
by expediting the necessary arrangements.

On 10 Ghinbot (18 May) the second University team, made up
of one person from the faculty, Ayele Tube (College of Business
Administration), one from the administration, Kebede Semegn
(Purchasing Department), and eight students left for Wello to distribute the first relief food to the victims of famine. The team was
led by the able organizer, Kebede Semegn. Although the team
encountered some difficulties with the police and the administration
in Dese, it managed to carry out its assigned duty of buying and
distributing grain to the starving people. The police and administration in Dese were very eager to get the cash from the team.[72]
The team had at its disposal an initial sum of 67,000 Birr, with

which it conducted the first organized large-scale grain distribution in the famine-stricken areas of Wello and elsewhere. The distribution of grain is shown in Table I.

TABLE I

DISTRIBUTION OF UNIVERSITY RELIEF GRAIN

Centre	Grain in Quintals	Number of Persons
Kombolcha	310	3000
Chelga	171	2700
Weldeya	700	8500
Doro Ghibir	321	3500
Qobbo	500	5650
Allamata	500	5200
Mersa	345	3400
Maichew	123	1428
Total	2970	33378

Source: Report of the University Team.

As indicated in the report of the team, this distribution did nothing more than raise the hopes of the starving hundreds of thousands. But it did also open the way for other organizations such as Telecommunications, Ethiopian Airlines, the Imperial Body Guard and the Army to follow the example of taking whatever contributions they had directly to the people, without going through the doubtful and slow governmental machinery. This fact was the boldest manifestation of a decisive vote of no confidence on the government. It may also be stated that such an action could not have been contemplated by many people in 1959, during the Tigray Famine.

The University continued to play a very important role in famine relief. The University Famine Relief and Rehabilitation Organization (U.F.R.R.O.) was established in 1974, and it is still active.[73]

The Parliament

On 20 Megabit, 1965 (29 March 1973), at the regular session of Parliament, representatives from Wello, citing an article from their rules of procedure, requested the president to take up the Wello

Famine as an urgent issue deserving priority over other items on the agenda for the day. The presiding chairman was clearly against this move, most probably with instructions from the government. When he saw that practically all the representatives were in favour of the motion and when they refused to discuss any other issue but the Wello Famine, the chairman simply declared the meeting adjourned and walked out. The representatives remained in their places, and without any chairman or discipline they unsuccessfully tried to discuss the issue. Exactly the same thing happened the following day. Having been informed earlier, Abraham Demoz and Mesfin Wolde-Mariam were there on both occasions. It was at this time that they realized that Parliament might not be as effective an instrument as they had expected. The decision to work for the formation of a fact-finding team was made after the two Parliamentary sessions that proved to be a fiasco.

The government muzzled Parliament for about fifteen days more. It was on 5 Miazia 1965 (13 April 1973) that the Wello Famine was allowed to be discussed in Parliament in the presence of some high-ranking government officials. One of the representatives from Wello stated that there were no less than 735,000 starving people in Wello, and exhibited some photographs as evidence of the severity of the famine. The same government official who spoke on television almost two months earlier spoke in Parliament, too, rejecting the figure quoted and the photographs not only as "lies but also something that exposes the country" to vicious propaganda. The truth, according to him, was that the problem "was not serious enough to warrant a request for international assistance."[74]

It may be recalled that the University fact-finding team left for Wello the next day, on 6 Miazia (14 March), and found conditions in Wello, from Kembolcha to Weldeya, extremely agonizing. At any rate, Parliament merely served the government officials to express their "no-problem" illusion. Was it really an illusion?

The Government

Clearly, the government was under some sort of pressure from February onwards to recognize the serious problem of famine in Wello. This pressure came mostly from the University and Parliament. It is important to note that it *did react* to these pressures, but absolutely negatively and ferociously. But why did it not address itself to the real issue, the problem of famine? Was it an illusion or outright denial of the truth they knew very well? How did they expect to hide mass death?

As already been pointed out earlier, documents exist to prove that government officials from *wereda* level to the Prime Minister and the Emperor knew or had the opportunity to know about the imminent Wello Famine long before it turned into a mass killer, especially of women, children and old people. The more evidence was presented to the government the more vehemently it denied the real problem of famine. It appears, and it is in fact demonstrable, that the whole bureaucracy had developed the art of sifting information in order to make it acceptable to higher authorities. The higher the information moved, the more it lost its original, crude and unpleasant conformity with the reality.[75]

Only two days before Parliament attempted to put the Wello Famine on its agenda, on 18 Megabit 1965 (27 March 1973), the government appointed its own fact-finding team made up of junior officials. Starting on 22 Megabit (31 March), the team visited various places and examined some documents in Dese. On 4 Miazia, one day before the discussion of the issue in Parliament, the team sent its report. Although the magnitude and the severity had certainly escaped it, the team did recognize the problem. This is obvious from its report, in which it requested 6,000 quintals cf grain for 55,000 needy people, as well as some powdered milk and special food for 2,000 children.[76] Presumably, it was with such information in his hands that the senior government official totally rejected not only the statements made but also the photographs presented by one of the representatives from Wello as "lies." The truth is that the government had even more and better information on the Wello Famine.

The Ministry of Interior had received a rather detailed report with figures of deaths and emigration for some *awrajas* from the Governor-General in Dese. Copies of this report were also sent to the Ministry of Finance, Ministry of Community Development and Social Affairs, Ministry of Agriculture and Ministry of Public Health.[77]

It must be noted that although the government had received a more detailed and more accurate report from the Governor-General of Wello a day before Parliament discussed the Wello issue, they chose to ignore it and persist in their denial. Moreover, the government's own fact-finding team had also sent its final report on Wello

TABLE II

DETAILS OF DEATHS IN AND EMIGRATION FROM THREE *Awrajas* IN
WELLO, 1973

Awrajas	1	2	3	4	5	6	7	8	9
Borena Sayint	1016	5024	1410	1775	8210	798	19	10869	5068
Werre-Himeno	94	574	156	258	988	412	66	11425	2373
Wadla-Delanta	651	1355	940	1022	3317	235	14	14362	1501
Total	1761	6954	2506	3055	12515	1445	99	36656	8942

1. Abandoned houses.
2. Number of males who left for another place.
3. Number of women who left.
4. Number of children who left.
5. Total number of persons that left their villages.
6. Number of livestock sold.
7. Number of persons who died.
8. Number of livestock that died.
9. Number of persons suffering from illness.

Source: Report of the Governor-General of Wello (Reference *77*).

before it proceeded to Tigray on 5 Miazia (13 April). In this report, the team not only included an explanation of natural and socio-economic roots of famine, but also considerably raised its earlier estimate of the number of persons in need of immediate assistance. Now, it requested 75,000 quintals of grain for 300,000 persons and special food for 36,520 children.[78] Even these figures, however, amounted to only one-half of the estimated number of 738,285 given in the report of the Governor-General.

Still the government remained unconvinced, or at least it appeared to be so. On 16 Miazia (24 April) the Emperor sent a senior Minister to Wello. On the same day the Amharic daily newspaper *Addis Zemen* reported for the first time that 10,000 quintals of grain had been sent to Wello and northern Shewa to help victims of "drought". It was on 19 Miazia (27 April) that the same newspaper reported the request for assistance from friendly countries and international organizations.

If the government appeared to be dissatisfied or doubtful about the verbal description of the conditions in Wello, it had very little reason to doubt the authenticity and the gravity of the problem as depicted by the television cameraman, Elias Birru, who made a film on Wello, in April 1973, six months before the one made by Jonathan Dimbleby. This film was seen by only five senior officials of the government.[79]

With all this evidence in their hands, the government officials continued to be irritated by any factual description of the conditions in Wello. Various ministries gave press releases in an obvious attempt to falsify newspaper reports abroad. Moreover, through the Ethiopian Embassy in London, they made a serious attempt to prevent the showing of Dimbleby's film.[80]

There should be no doubt, therefore, that the Imperial Ethiopian Government did its best, even against extreme odds, to conceal the Wello Famine. By the simple utilitarian criterion of John Stuart Mill—"Actions are right in proportion as they tend to promote happiness, wrong as they tend to produce the reverse of happiness"[81] —it will not be difficult to declare the Imperial Government's action on the Wello Famine absolutely wrong.

NOTES

[1]Richard Pankhurst, *The Great Ethiopian Famine of 1888-1892, op. cit.*

[2]Richard Pankhurst, "The History of Famine and Pestilence in Ethiopia Prior to the Founding of Gonder", *Journal of Ethiopian Studies*, Vol X., No. 2, Addis Ababa, July 1972.

[3]Richard Pankhurst, "The Earliest History of Famine and Pestilence in Ethiopia: A Note of the Egyptian Deaths", *Ethiopian Medical Journal*, Vol. 11. No. 3, Addis Ababa, 1973.

[4]"The History of Famine . . .", *op. cit.*, pp. 42-43.

[5]*Ibid.*, pp. 44-45.

[6]*Ibid.*, pp. 45-46.

[7]*Ibid.*, pp. 49-52.

[8]*Ibid.*, pp. 52-63.

[9]Richard Pankhurst, *The Great Ethiopian Famine . . ., op. cit.*, p. 2.

[10]Richard Pankhurst, *The Great Ethiopian Famine . . ., op. cit.*, p. 6.

[11]Aleqa Atsme, *The History of the Gallas* (An Amharic manuscript, Addis Ababa, 1911).

[12]Quoted by R. Pankhurst in *The Great Ethiopian Famine . . . , op. cit.*, pp. 44-45.

[13]28/11/50. All official government correspondence is in Amharic and, when quoted, it is my own translation. Documents are referred to by dates only, in Ethiopian calendar.

[14]Tigray to the Ministry of Interior, 3/13/50.

[15]Red Cross to the Ministry of Interior, 10/6/51.

[16]Ministry of Interior of Red Cross, 10/6/51.

[17]Gamo Gofa to the Ministry of Interior, 27/1/52.

[18]Ministry of Interior to Gamo Gofa, 30/2/52.

[19]Jarra *Awraja* to the Ministry of Interior, 27/3/52.

[20]Ministry of Palace to Ministry of Interior, 25/3/52.

[21]Public Security to Ministry of Interior, 10/5/53.

[22]Shewa to Kembata *Awraja*, 5/13/53.

[23]M.P. from Kembata to Parliament, 3/4/45.

[24]Prime Minister's Office of Ministry of Interior, 18/8/53.

[25]Agent of Ministry of Agriculture in Tigray to Ministry of Agriculture, 2/13/53, 15/1/54.

[26]For discussion on the details, see Chapter Three of this book.

[27]Telegram, Tigray to Ministry of Interior, 18/11/50.

[28]Tigray to Ministry of Interior, 26/1/51.

[29]Police Head Quarter to Public Security, 22/1/51.

[30]Adwa *Awraja* to Tigray, 11/2/51, Tigray to the Ministry of Interior, 2/6/52.

[31]Tigray to the Ministry of Interior, 28/2/51.

[32]Police Head Quarter to the Ministry of Interior, 4/2/57,

[33]Ministry of Agriculture to the Ministry of Interior, 18/3/57.

[34]Ministry of Interior to Wello, 24/3/57.

[35]Wello to Ministry of Interior, 11/6/57.

[36]Ministry of Interior to Wello, 30/10/57.

[37]Wello to Ministry of Interior, 27/11/57.

[38]Dese *Awraja* to Wello, 18/12/57.

[39]Ministry of Interior to Wello, 4/2/58.

[40]Ministry of Pen to Ministry of Finance, 27/1/58.

[41]Wello to Ministry of Interior, 22/1/58.

[42]Transport Company to Grain Board, 7/3/58.

[43]Wello to the Ministry of Interior, 24/4/58.

[44]Wello to Ministry of Interior, 18/5/58. Same to same, 26/7/58.

[45]Wag *Awraja* Police to Wag *Awraja*, 24/11/58.

[46]Petition of the People of Lasta *Awraja* to the Ministry of Interior, 19/7/58.

[47]M.P. of Wag *Awraja* to the Ministry of Interior, 8/8/58.

[48]Lasta *Awraja* Police to Wello Police, 29/11/58.

[49]Wag *Awraja* Police to Wello Police, 30/12/58.

[50]Wag *Awraja* to Wello, 12/1/59.

[51]Elders of Lasta to Ministry of Interior, 19/7/58.

[52]Grain Board to Wello, 6/10/59.

[53]Telegram, Wag *Awraja* to Ministry of Interior, 3/2/60.

[54]Wag *Awraja* Ministry of Interior, 26/11/60.

[55]Ministry of Interior to Ministry of Agriculture, 24/7/60.

[56]Awsa *Awraja* to Ministry of Interior, 18/7/59.

[57]Council of Ministers to Ministry of Interior, 9/4/61.

[58]Ministry of Agriculture to Ministry of Interior, 12/11/61.

[59]Oral information acquired in Dese.

[60]Much has been written on Famine in Ethiopia since 1974. Even the same people have written many times. See, for instance, Mehari Gebre-Medhin, "Famine in Ethiopia", *Ethiopian Medical Journal,* Vol. 12, No. 2, Addis Ababa, 1974; Shewandagn Belete, Mehari Gebre-Medhin, Bantirgu Haile Mariam, Mario Maffi, Bo Vahlquist and Zewdie Wolde-Gebriel, "Famine in Ethiopia: A Study of Shelter Population in the Wello Region", *Courier*, Vol. XXVI, 1976; Mehari Gebre-Medhin and Bo Vahlquist, "Famine in Ethiopia—A Brief Review", *The American Journal of Clinical Nutrition* 29; September 1976, Ed. Bo Vahlquist, *Famine in Ethiopia*, Monograph No. 48, Environmental Child Health, Institute of Nutrition, Uppasala University, Feb. 1977; Mehari Gebre-Medhin and Bo Vahlquist "Famine in Ethiopia—The Period 1973-75", *Nutrition Reviews*, Vol. 35, No. 18, August 1977. A completely different work based on some examination of Ethiopian institutions in relation to famine is Karl Johan Lundstrom's *Northeastern Ethiopia: Society in Famine: A Study of Three Institutions in a Period of Severe Strain*, Research Report No. 34, Scandinavian Institute of African Studies (Uppsala, 1976).

[61]Commission of Inquiry, *The Details of the Wello Famine,*(in Amharic, Addis Ababa, Tiqimt 1968).

[62]Wello parliamentarians to the Emperor, 28/2/65.

[63]Commission of Inquiry, *op. cit.*, pp. 41-43.

[64]Proclamation of 10/3/65.

[65]Jack Shepherd, *The Politcs of Starvation* (New York, 1975), p. xii. It must, incidentally, be mentioned that the appointment of Seyoum Gebre Egziabher, Solomon Inquay and Mesfin Wolde-Mariam (all three faculty members of the University) to various posts outside Addis Ababa is true, but these appointments had nothing to do with the famine. The three professors that went to Wello to investigate the famine are not the ones mentioned by Jack Shepherd, p. 16.

[66]Proclamation of 19/3/65.

[67]Minutes of meeting of Emperor, the Prime Minister, nine Ministers and the Governor-General, 21/8/65.

[68]The Report of the Minister of the Interior to the Emperor, 30/8/65. This report, although not in any sense realistic, was much nearer to the situation in Wello than his verbal report (f.n. 67 above).

[69]Commission of Inquiry, *op. cit.*, p. 61.

[70]*Loc. cit.*

[71]*Ibid.*, p. 63.

[72]For details of this encounter with the police, that for all practical purposes amounted to arrest, see the report of the team (in Amharic), HSIU Relief Aid to Famine Victims (Addis Ababa, E.C. Ghinbot 10-Sene 12, 1965).

[73]For a survey of relief organizations see U.F.R.R.O., *Survey of Famine Relief and Rehabilitation Organizations and Agencies in Ethiopia* (Addis Ababa, December 1974).

[74]Commission of Inquiry, *op. cit.*, p. 82.

[75]See f.n. 68 above.

[76]Commission of Inquiry, *op. cit.*, pp. 64-73.

[77]Report from the Governor-General Wello to the Ministry of Interior, Miazia 2, 1965 (in Amharic).

[78]Commission of Inquiry, *op. cit.*, p. 71.

[79]*Ibid.*, p. 83.

[80]*Ibid.*, pp. 105-8.

[81]*Utilitarianism, Liberty, and Representative Government* (Everyman's Library, 1948), p. 6.

Chapter Three

The Consequences of Famine

Provided there are records, it is simple enough to estimate the loss of human lives and livestock, and the loss of material property and investment, as well as the value of forestalled production. But the damage wrought by famine is much more than just that. When the peasants, who have nothing in store and who have staked all the future on their small plots of land that have failed to meet their minimum expectations for subsistence, experience crop failure, there is hopelessness that makes a human being empty to the core; there is helplessness that tortures a human being standing face to face with slow but certain death; there is pain and there is sorrow. Peasants in such a situation suffer not only starvation but also the humiliation of nothingness, neglected and forgotten in their misery. These costs are impossible to estimate. It is impossible to estimate in money value the daily helpless suffering of the mother whose pain of hunger is compounded by the innocently persistent demands of her children. It is impossible to estimate in money value the tearless cries and the wrinkled faces of starving children. Day by day, misery is compounded by the debilitating process of starvation.

Spatial dislocation and the accompanying dismemberment of families also falls into this non-monetary dimension of famine. Very often men are separated from their wives and children, and from their kith and kin. This tearing and shattering of the social fabric has a social and psychological impact that may linger for years. In fact, there is good reason to believe that the process of social dislocation and dismemberment initiated by famine will eventually lead to dehumanization and social disorganization. It is not very difficult to comprehend that people left helplessly on their own to face famine soon learn that all social values are fairy tales, the only thing of real value being that of survival. This painful experience may ultimately affect an entire society, perhaps even all humanity.

Human Mortality Due to Famine

It is impossible to have a correct estimate of the human deaths due to famine in the whole twenty years under consideration. Information gathered from official documents is clearly incomplete. We have quantitative information on famine-affected population for 121 *awraja* famine years, totalling 6,478,760, or an average of 53,543 per *awraja* famine year. On the basis of this average, the total famine-affected population during the twenty years comes to 25,111,887, which is practically the same as the total rural population of the country. But, of course, the figure relates only to those *awrajas* that have suffered famine, some for many years.

Information from official sources on number of deaths due to famine is available only for 63 *awraja* famine years out of a total of 469; and general statements of famine deaths for an additional 23 *awraja* famine years. For the 63 *awraja* famine years for which we have some figures, the total number of deaths comes to 34,406, or an average of 562 deaths per *awraja* famine year. If we apply this average for the total number of famine years, 469, we get 263,578 deaths, a figure which is much lower than the actual death rate.[1]

This gross underestimation of famine deaths may be explained in several ways. In the first place, the government officials, especially at the district level, have neither the capacity nor the means to gather the information and express it in quantitative terms. For most of them, 1,000 is infinity. In the second place, bureaucratic caution dictates that it is very unwise to be precise. In the third place, if and when they are precise and give exact figures of deaths, the prompt request from the Ministry of Interior is for the names and addresses of the dead, a laborious work, the issue of famine being shelved as secondary. Sometimes the Ministry of Interior even requests evidence to prove that the reported deaths are in fact due to famine. One exasperated district official replying to such a request wrote with bitter sarcasm: "Am I to carry a corpse to Addis Ababa as a proof?"

Some unofficial estimates, however, exist for some famines in some *awrajas.* In Wag *Awraja* alone, for example, in the famine of 1966-1968 between 45,000 and 60,000 persons died, according to one report.[2] In 1973, in only five *awrajas* of Wello, it was estimated that 106,000 persons died of famine,[3] or 20% of the estimated population. If we apply the 20% mortality rate to all the twelve *awrajas* of Wello, using the population estimate of the Central Statistical Office for that year, we get 437,460. The official estimate of deaths for the Wello Famine is 16,000, although it is admitted to be incomplete. We may take the rates computed by the Ethiopian Nutrition Institute (ENI) (*Table III*) as a general guide.

The Tigray Famine of 1958-1960, although it was never televised and hardly even publicised, was in no way less than the Wello Famine of 1973. There is reason to believe that the population of Tigray in 1958 was 1,961,000, and, again applying the same mortality rate as that of Wello, we find that about 397,000 persons might have died. Tigray suffered seriously again in 1973, with perhaps 200,000 deaths. This means that, in Tigray and Wello alone, a total of about 700,000 to 1,100,000 persons might have died between 1953 and 1974.

TABLE III
AGE-SPECIFIC DEATH RATES
(*per thousand*)

Age Groups	Male	Female	Both Sexes
<1	567	667	619
1—4	477	636	542
5—14	154	131	143
15—44	130	70	97
45—64	299	147	217
>65	400	258	331
All Ages	216	165	190

Source: Profile of Wello under Famine, 1974.

We can try another way. If we take our figure of 25,111,887 for the famine-affected population, at the rate of 20% we get 5,022,377 deaths over the twenty-year period. This may be considered a bit too high, but even one-half of that figure is an immense loss. According to the Central Statistical Office, the average crude death rate for the country is 19.8 per 1000.[4] If we apply this rate for each *awraja*, annual deaths per *awraja* may roughly be about 5,000. Again if we assume a rate of 5,000 deaths per *awraja* famine year, since there were 469 *awraja* famine years we get 2,345,000 deaths. Even this appears low when we remember that in Tigray and Wello alone between 700,000 and 1,100,000 must have died in the famines of 1958-61 and 1973-75 in Tigray, in 1966-68 in Lasta and Wag, and in the whole of Wello in 1973-75. But a year-by-year careful estimate of deaths for each *awraja* gives a total of 3,954,000 deaths. We may therefore assume that famine deaths in Ethiopia in the twenty years may be between two and five million.

Emigration Due to Famine

The spatial dislocation of large numbers of people is another important consequence of famine. In the official documents, figures on emigration are available for seven years and for only twelve *awrajas*. The total figure for emigration amounts to 43,596. This is certainly a ridiculously low figure, even less accurate than the official records of deaths. The survey that was made by the Ethiopian Nutrition Institute in five *awrajas* of Wello in 1974 indicates that the average rate of emigration was about 8%, amounting to 46,720 persons. For all the twelve *awrajas* of Wello the figure will rise to 174,984. If we take 8% of the famine-affected population of 25,111,887, the number of emigrants will be 2,008,951. If it may be reasonable to assume that, in any famine, the number of persons emigrating will be much more than the number that die, this figure is certainly too low; it is only about one-half to equal to the number of estimated deaths. But we must remember that, perhaps, a large proportion of those who died may have been on their way to some other place, away from their villages. Famine deaths and famine emigration are not mutually exclusive. Famine mortality cannot be determined only from the source, nor can emigration.

In connection with emigration, three points need to be stressed. First, most emigrants are relatively young men whose departure from their farms tends to perpetuate and intensify famine for the weak, the young and the old, together with the women left behind. Second, the demographic imbalance created in both the areas of origin and destination eventually becomes a source of numerous social problems. Before the 1973 famine, the male-female ratio in Wello was 115:100, but after the famine it became 89:100.[5] During the same time the proportion of those less than 15 years of age dropped from 63.8% to 56.2%, and of those under 5 from 17.6% to 11%.[6] Third, the emigrants who arrive in large numbers in another area create economic and socio-political problems by sparking regional and ethnic feelings and by generating fear of exhausting local resources. In many parts of Ethiopia, many starving emigrants were killed by local people who wanted to protect their land reserves.

Loss of Livestock

During the most widely publicized famine of 1973, a number of surveys were conducted in various parts of the country. These give us a clue to the tremendous loss of livestock in the country. In only five *awrajas* of Wello, one report states:

> On the whole, 93% of the sheep, 90% of the cows, 86% of the goats, 72% of the oxen, 90% of the camels, 60% of the donkeys and 95% of the mules have died.[7]

This loss refers to the time before April 1974. Another report, referring to the period between September 1974, and February 1975, states that 66% of the cattle, 11% of the sheep and goats and 72% of the camels had died.[8] In Elkerre, half of the cows, goats, sheep and camels, and two-fifths of the oxen, horses, donkeys and mules died during the period between September 1973 and September 1974. For the most part, these livestock deaths are attributed to drought, but also lions and hyenas have had their share.[9] In the Ogaden the situation was similarly bad, since it was found that "the average cattle-holding per family in the southern Ogaden has fallen from 15.9/head to 6.1/head" by December 1974.[10]

Practically all the reports give the livestock loss in percentages without any reference to absolute numbers. Since estimates of livestock numbers by *awraja* are available, it is not difficult to estimate livestock mortality in absolute terms. An attempt to assess the loss in money, however, ran into hundreds of thousands of Birr, and it appeared such an incredibly exaggerated loss for such a poor country that it was thought better to omit it altogether. Normally livestock resources are not converted into cash for any sort of calculation, and that is partly the reason why the loss of livestock in cash appears unrealistic.

There is, however, a very important point that is worth mentioning. It may sound paradoxical that human beings and livestock die simultaneously by starvation. Why, we may ask, do people die of famine instead of surviving the hard times by slaughtering and eating their cattle, sheep and goats, and camels? Even the skins of these animals could fetch good prices in the market. Would this not have saved many human lives? Why do people and livestock die of famine together?[11] For the moment we can only speculate on the answer.

Perhaps it is important to understand the life-style and the attitudes and value systems of the peasants and nomadic pastoralists. The Ethiopian peasants view their livestock as a form of capital, as instruments of production, and as savings. For the nomadic pastoralists, livestock mean even more, since they are considered as the only basis of life. Without livestock, the peasants have nothing to rely on for the farm work that they must hope to continue in the future. The pastoralists' dependence on livestock is so total that they consider them almost beyond value. In the southern part of the Awash Valley, for example, there is a group of pastoralists that illustrates this special value attached to livestock. This group of pastoralists is called *Rebbin Qelle*, meaning literally "unless God kills" that is to say, the group never deliberately kills cattle, sheep, goats, or camels for any purpose. They eat meat only when "God kills" the animals. Whatever may be said about the risk to health, this pastoral belief raises livestock to a level of sacredness and assures their natural increase.

So, even at a time of crisis, to slaughter animals and to use them for food will mean obliterating any hope of a revival in the future. It is, perhaps, this hope for a better future in an absolutely hopeless situation, and the realization, as the peasants and pastoralists see it, that their future is dependent on livestock that prevents them from consuming animals for present needs. As the peasants see it, perhaps, one should muddle through present danger rather than extending it into the future. In a sense, the future, more remote and known as well as unpredictable, may appear to them more frightening and more hazardous than the present which they confront with helpless bravery. This interpretation of their reluctance to slaughter livestock to save their lives injects into their scheme of valuation a strong element of concern for the future in face of present danger. The paradox, however, is that, when they consume poisonous crops under pressure of starvation, it seems that present danger is more real than future risk. Is this a real or only an apparent contradiction? We shall come back to this question later.

A careful analysis of the data of the livestock that died or were sold, eaten or stolen reveals a significant point to support the statements made in the previous paragraph.

In 1974, when the disastrous consequences of famine had reached its peak, the proportion of livestock that died in Wello was almost four times as much as the proportion that were sold (*Table IV*).[12] In Harerghe, too, the situation was almost the same (*Table V*).[13] It is interesting to note, however, the difference between the two regions. In the case of the pastoralists of Harerghe there is hardly any difference between the average proportion of the cattle, sheep and goats, and camels that died, or were sold, on one hand, and the proportion of draught animals that died, or were sold, on the other. But in the case of the peasant cultivators of Wello, the average proportion of cattle, sheep and goats and camels that died was more than ten times as much as the proportion of those that were sold, while for draught animals the proportions of those that died and of those sold were much closer.

TABLE IV

COMPARISON OF LIVESTOCK SALES AND MORTALITY, %
WELLO, 1974

Livestock	Sold	Died	Other	Retained	Total
Oxen	19	71	2	8	100
Cows	7	89	1	3	100
Camels	1	88	5	6	100
Sheep & Goats	6	89	1	4	100
Average	8.25	84.25	2.25	5.25	100
Horses	38	26	12	24	100
Mules	29	41	6	24	100
Donkeys	24	56	0	20	100
Average	30.33	41.00	6.00	22.67	100
Average of Total	17.7	65.7	3.9	12.7	100

Source: Profile of Wello under Famine, 1974.

TABLE V
COMPARISON OF LIVESTOCK SALES AND MORTALITY, %,
HARERGHE, 1974

Livestock	Sold	Died	Other	Retained	Total
Cattle	13	50	?	?	63
Sheep & Goats	19	56	?	?	75
Camels	4	42	?	?	46
Average	12	49	?	?	61
Donkey & Mules	11	46	?	?	57
Average of Total	12	49	?	?	61

Source: Harerghe under Drought, 1974, p. 47.

The fact that a greater proportion of livestock died in both regions than the proportion sold is easier to understand than the differences in the sizes of the proportions themselves. It seems difficult to infer from the differences that peasant cultivators value livestock more, or have a lesser tendency to consider livestock as a disposable commodity, than pastoralists.

In general, however, the indications we get from the figures in Tables IV and V seem to confirm the view that both peasants and pastoralists attach an incredibly high value to cattle, sheep, goats and camels, a much higher value than to donkeys, mules and horses. The fact that, even in extreme crisis, subsistence producers are reluctant to part with their livestock may appear to be irrational to those who are not in their condition. We shall come back to this question in a little while.

Land

As we shall see later, land is not a mere object to the Ethiopian peasants. Consequently, the proportion of peasants who actually sold their land is rather low. The average number of families that "sold or abandoned" their land in the six *awrajas* in Wello is only about 15.3%. The highest proportion was 27.5% in Ambassel, and no land was sold in Lasta.[14] The proportion of families that mortgaged their land is even less, the average being only 2.6%.[15] Evidently, nearly 85% of the peasants, on the average, preserved their right over the land, whatever its utility. As one peasant expressed it, the general belief is that "death is inevitable and, therefore, it is better to die with one's honour without giving cause to the future generation to curse" him.[16] But we shall return to this point later.

Disruption of Agricultural Production

Perhaps the most devastating consequence of famine is that it is self-perpetuating. The normal process of agricultural activity is arrested due to the decimation of the oxen, lack of seed, and considerable reduction of manpower. The lack of harvest in 1973 was attributed to loss of oxen by 44.2% of the peasants in Ambassel *Awraja* 87% in Qallu, 100% in Awsa, 84.1% in Rayya and Qobbo, and 68% in Yejju. Lack of seed was the main reason that prevented farm work for 7.8% of the peasants in Ambassel, 11% in Qallu, and about 1% in Rayya and Qobbo.[17] The remainder gave shortage of rainfall as their main reason for not cultivating. In 1974 and 1975, again the reduced harvests were at least partly attributed to shortage of oxen and seed, although army worms, other insects, and rodents were also important causes.[18]

The slow and grinding action of famine which perhaps originates in one poor harvest starts a process that reduces the harvest of subsequent years. Famine prolongs and intensifies famine. The effect of famine on people and livestock, especially oxen, is to reduce drastically the available work force, which in turn affects the land. It means that all the three factors of production are adversely affected by famine, crippling agricultural production so effectively that it promotes famine on a much wider scale and more intensely.

In money terms the damage wrought by famine is enormous, even for a poor country like Ethiopia. A preliminary and rough estimate of the damage for only the four national famines runs into billions of Birr.

Long-range Consequences of Famine

The social, political, and economic damages wrought by famine as well as the mass deaths have been the subject of much writing. But there are other effects of famine that have not received the attention they deserve. This is perhaps because the most immediate shocking effects of famine are so overwhelming that attention is focussed on saving lives and rehabilitating the survivors. This attention, however, soon subsides, leaving the poor surviving victims to their own fate. These surviving victims bear the physical and psychological scars of famine, and may be impaired for the rest of their lives.

Under the agonizing pressure of starvation, people eat roots or leaves as "emergency foods". They may have no prior knowledge of whether these roots and leaves are poisonous.[19] There are reports, indeed, that many people have died of poisonous plants consumed as food. Sometimes they consume poisonous infected grain, we have every reason to believe, knowingly.[20] The consumption of grain infected by ergot is such a case. The peasants have given this poisonous grain a name that succinctly describes its debilitating effects: they call it *libb aqilt* or "heart-melting". The consumption of this grain produces stomach-ache, headache, nausea, diarrhoea, twitching and numbness, and even insanity, ultimately incapacitating the hands and legs before it kills.[21] The study made by the Ethiopian Nutrition Institute (ENI) in two sub-districts in Lasta *Awraja* shows that 47 persons died and 93 were seriously ill of ergotism.[22] In addition, some 40 to 50 infants below the age of four died because their mothers ceased to be lactiferous as a result of ergotism.[23]

A more or less similar problem ensues from the consumption of a special of pea, *Lathyrus sativus*, which causes neurolathyrism, a disease that affects the nervous system.[24] Here again this dangerous pulse is given an apt name, *sebbere* or "breaker" or "paralyser."[25] A study conducted in three sub-districts in three different *awrajas* in Gonder found 1,374 cases of neurolathyrism.[26]

Why would people eat crops to which they have given terrifying names? Is it a form of suicide? An equally perplexing question was raised earlier: Why do people *and* livestock starve to death *together*? Why don't starving people turn their livestock into food during the famine period? Undoubtedly, these are questions that require a separate and different kind of research. At the moment we can only speculate.

The special attachment that peasants and pastoralists have to their livestock has already been indicated. But the questions we posed in connection with livestock imply that they are disposable forms of wealth or a means of consumption. This is our perception, which is not necessarily shared by the peasants and pastoralists. A second implication that runs through all the questions is an element of choice. We assume that the peasants and pastoralists in a situation of famine have a choice between two neatly delineated alternatives: to consume, *or* not to consume their livestock; to consume, *or* not to consume the harmful crops.

For the famine-stricken subsistence producers who are experiencing the incessant torture of starvation, the alternatives are perhaps neither clearly delineated nor simple. How can they delineate the agonizing reality of the present from their faint hope for the future? Perhaps the subsistence producers perceive their livestock as their only link with the future and as an embodiment of their faint hope. Their livestock represent the seeds they must buy and the animal power they must need for their future farm work. To slaughter their livestock in order to alleviate their starvation may give them only short-lived satisfaction, while it obliterates any hope for recovery. Without their livestock they may perhaps feel convinced that present misery will be compounded with anxiety about a tolerable future that recedes beyond their reach. Hope against hope rather than hopelessness appears to be the driving force of subsistence producers in a famine situation.

The rationality of their actions must be viewed in the context of famine as well as in their condition of helplessness and isolation. Which is more rational to a starving family that may not have eaten for months—to starve to death, or to risk eating the harmful crops? Which is more rational to a starving family—to consume their livestock and ensure the prolongation of the famine period, or to preserve that capital as the foundation of future recovery? In both the cases the alternatives are distressful and involve much anguish.

The apparent contradiction between the preservation of the livestock as an indication of concern for the future and the eating of the harmful crops as a lack of that concern may be understood in terms of hope. It is, perhaps, the strength of their hope against hope that enables them to face bravely the slow and daily march to death by starvation *with* their livestock, as it may be the same hope against hope that gives them the courage to eat the harmful crops and to risk their crippling effect. What Wordsworth said of love may also be true of hope:

There is a comfort in the strength of love;
'Twill make a thing endurable which else
Would overset the brain, or break the heart.

The power of life asserts itself equally over the present danger and future risk, making bearable what normally appears unbearable.

It will be idle to expect anything different from a subsistence production system. Where the socio-economic and political organization is sensitive to the dangers of famine, arrangements can easily be made to buy the livestock at reasonable prices and to provide food at subsidized rates, ensuring, at the same time, future recovery. In a subsistence production system, such arrangements are not envisaged by the government; and if they are, they will not be accepted by the subsistence producers who have no faith in the socio-economic and political institutions. The subsistence producers are, therefore, alone in their misery and have to attempt to get themselves out of it into a relatively better future.

There are other effects of famine, effects that the victims cannot be aware of. Perhaps the most serious long-range consequence of famine is brain damage.

> Growth of the brain, as with any other tissue, results from the multiplication of cells during growth periods before and often soon after birth. This growth of living tissue cannot occur if the necessary nutrient materials are not available.[27]

And explaining the effects of early malnutrition, Balagura writes:

> Severe early malnutrition in human infants leads to smaller body frames and lower body weight, smaller brains, lower intelligence quotients, and a decreased capacity to perform in various types of psychological tests. This is true of malnourished children all over the world, including the United States. The performance level of malnourished children can be improved by careful nutritional rehabilitation programs, but only when their malnutrition occurred after they were 1 or 2 years of age. The retardation caused by malnutrition does not improve if the period of malnourishment occurred during the first months of life.[28]

There is no reason to doubt these statements that are supported by numerous experiments on animals and observations on humans. Referring to a more specific case of malnutrition, Balagura states that, even "though experiments in maternal malnutrition cannot be performed on humans, society unfortunately provides us with a number of human cases that replicate in almost every detail the laboratory work done with rats".[29]

The fact that famine, as the most extreme form of malnutrition, stunts the physical and mental development of children does not seem debatable.[30] The effect of famine on children must be understood not only in its interference in the normal biological process of growth and development, but also in terms of the psychological scars that it is bound to leave on their minds.

These facts lead us into a realm of speculation: All other things remaining equal, will surviving famine victims develop a production capacity that will enable them to live a life that is free from famine? Or will they become even more vulnerable to famine? Perhaps there are no conclusive answers to these questions. But the available evidence seems to indicate that famine may linger in coming; once it arrives, however, the probability that it will recur is very high. Out of the 95 *awrajas* that have had famine, only 10 did not have a second famine period during the twenty years. In fact it can be stated with confidence that, insofar as the Ethiopian experience is concerned, the onset of a severe famine seems to ensure that sooner or later more severe famine will follow. In the twenty-year period, no severe famine has failed to repeat itself. Of course, this need not be the case in the future.

It is important, therefore, to bear in mind the most difficult and more complex problem of the effects of famine on the physical and mental capacities of the victims together with the social, economic and political consequences of famine.

The Cost of Relief

The cost of relief, which invariably arrives too late, is very high. Between 1973 and 1979, from the Federal Republic of Germay alone, Ethiopia received 172.6 million Birr in relief aid coming from government and private sources.[31] The United States of America provided sorghum and wheat at a cost of 5.6 million dollars in 1959, 4.3 million in 1961, 0.3 million in 1964, 4.8 million in 1965, 0.3 million in 1966, 0.8 million in 1969, adding up to a total of over 15 million dollars for the six years. From 1970 to 1978 a further 50 million dollars was given by the United States of America.[32] All in all, between 1959 and 1978, the United States of America gave Ethiopia 65 million dollars, or about 150 million Birr, in relief aid. The total external aid for 1973-1979 is shown in Table VI. Although it has not been possible to find the exact cost

TABLE VI
RELIEF AID TO ETHIOPIA, 1973-1979

Donor	Birr	Percentage
Governments	407.42	56.21
Inter Governmental	116.74	15.28
International Voluntary Agencies	77.40	10.63
UN Organizations	129.21	17.83
Total	724.77	100.00

Source: Relief and Rehabilitation Commission.

to the Ethiopian government, there can be no doubt that it is very high. Moreover, the Ethiopian civil servants, workers and businessmen have made tremendous contributions, especially after the revolution.

NOTES

[1]C.S.O., *The Demography of Ethiopia: Results of the National Sample Survey*, Second Round (Addis Ababa, January, 1974), Vol. 1, p. 71.

[2]Chairman of Wage Relief Committee.

[3]*Profile of Wello under Famine, op. cit.*, p. 26.

[4]C.S.O., *The Demography of Ethiopia, op. cit.*, p. 71.

[5]*Ibid.*, p. xiv.

[6]*Ibid.*, p. ii.

[7]*Profile of Wello under Famine, op. cit.*, p. 30.

[8]RRC, Consolidated Food & Nutrition Information System, *Wello: Two Years After the Crisis*, (Addis Ababa, September 1975), p. 39.

[9]ENI, *Food and Nutrition Survey, Bale* (Addis Ababa, August 1974), p. 21.

[10]RRC, Consolidated Food & Nutrition Information System, *Report of First Round Surveilance, Ogaden, Harerghe* (Addis Ababa, November-December 1974), p. 18.

[11]It is even strange that this question, to my knowledge, has never been asked. It is obviously a question that requires special investigation. In view of the fact that the preparation of dried meat is one of the arts of Ethiopian food culture, it would be odd to believe that it is forgotten at a time of extreme crisis.

[12]*Profile of Wello under Famine, op. cit.*, p. 125.

[13]RRC (John Seaman, Julius F.S. Holt, John P.W. Rivers), *Harerghe under Drought: A Survey of the Effects of Drought upon Human Nutrition in Harerghe Province* (Addis Ababa, May-June, 1974) p. 47.

[14]*Ibid.*, p. 35.

[15]*Loc. cit.*

[16]Verbal communication.

[17]*Ibid.*, p. 41.

[18]RRC, Consolidated Food & Nutrition Information System, *Wello: Two Years after the Crisis,* (Addis Ababa, September 1975), p. 12 and p. 32.

[19]Commission of Inquiry, *op. cit.*, p. 17.

[20]See, for instance, ENI (in Amharic), *A Report on Ergotism,* Addis Ababa, E.C. 1969.

[21]*Ibid.*, p. 4.

[22]*Ibid.*, p. 7.

[23]*Ibid.*, p. 8.

[24]Tesfaye Gebre-Ab, Zewdie Wolde-Gabriel, Mario Maffi, Zein Ahmed, Teklemariam Ayele, Haile Fanta, "Neurolathyrism—A Review and Report of an Epidemic," *Ethiopian Medical Journal,* Vol. 16, No. 1, Addis Ababa, 1978.

[25]*Ibid.*, p. 2.

[26]*Ibid.*, p. 6.

[27]Saul Balagura, *Hunger: A Biopsychological Analysis,* (New York, 1973), p. 153.

[28]*Ibid.*, pp. 155-56.

[29]*Ibid.*, p. 158.

[30]*Ibid.*, p. 156.

[31]Information acquired from the Embassy of the Federal Republic of Germany in Addis Ababa, December 1979.

[32]US AID/ETHIOPIA, *Program Operations Status Report as of 30 September 1978,* pp. 12-13.

PART III

VULNERABILITY TO FAMINE

Chapter Four

The Socio-Economic Conditions of Peasant Life

.

Possibilities and Limitations

It may be helpful to consider very briefly the problems felt by the peasants themselves before we take up the observations of outsiders. The peasants' perception of their own condition may give us a deeper insight into the problems of rural Ethiopia and help us compare the felt needs and perceptions in contrast to the assumed problems.

In a Rural Survey carried out by the Central Statistical Office, peasants were asked to state the reasons for not expanding their cultivated land. The Survey covered only 83 *awrajas,* and those that were left out were mostly the poorest ones.[1] The largest proportion of peasants, almost 42% gave lack of draught animals, i.e. mainly oxen, as their primary reason. The second largest proportion, about 32%, thought that land was not available. The third important reason, given by 17% was lack of manpower or labour. A fourth reason, given by only 4.5% of the peasants, was that the land was too poor. Perhaps, most significantly, a mere 0.3% of the peasants gave lack of market as a reason for not expanding their cultivated land.

It may be granted that the structured answers—lack of market, lack of manpower, lack of draught animals, land not available, land too poor, land too weedy—had already narrowed the scope of rural agricultural problems, even for the questions posed. Nevertheless, they do provide some insight for a better understanding of rural life. That lack of draught animals, lack of land, and shortage of labour come out as the three most important reasons constricting the expansion of farms is very enlightening. If we examine these answers for various parts of the country, some pattern seems to emerge.

Ignoring those *awrajas* that fall below the average, most of the *awrajas* that indicated labour shortage are in the southern half of the country. Six *awrajas* out of 24 in Tigray, Wello, Gojjam, and Gonder; 21 *awrajas* out of 27 in Wellega, Illubabor, Kefa, Gamo Gofa, and northern Sidamo; and 11 *awrajas* out of 25 in Shewa, Arsi, highland Bale and highland Harerghe indicated shortage of labour. Understandably, a higher proportion of peasants from the coffee-producing *awrajas* reported labour shortage as a factor constricting farm expansion.

Concerning shortage of draught animals, although the problem is relatively more diffused, it appears that the general pattern is reversed: 17 *awrajas* in Tigray, Wello, Gonder, and Gojjam; 14 *awrajas* in Wellega, Illubabor, Kefa, Gamo Gofa, and northern Sidamo; 8 *awrajas* in Shewa, highland Bale, and highland Harerghe indicated shortage of draught animals. Land shortage was reported from 12 *awrajas* in Tigray, Wello, Gojjam, and Gonder: from 5 *awrajas* in Sidamo alone; and from 14 *awrajas* in Shewa, highland Bale and highland Harerghe. Land that was too poor to be worth the effort is indicated by 13 *awrajas* in the north, 6 in the southwest, and 13 in the Shewa group.

As we shall soon see, the problems of peasant farming are not limited to shortages of land, labour and oxen, and to the poor quality of land. There is much evidence to indicate that the problem is not one of shortage but of organization and management as well as of incentives for higher productivity. The conclusions that we shall later draw from the observations of peasant farming may not correspond with what the peasants themselves perceive as indicated above.

The country has an area of approximately 1,200,000 square kilometres or 120,000,000 hectares. But the total cultivated land is only about 5,244,400 hectares[2] and perhaps some 300,000 hectares of government farms. This means that only about 5% of the total area is under cultivation. Excluding the more rugged land with steep slopes, land that is over 2,600 metres above sea level and land that receives less than 800 mm of annual rainfall, there is perhaps some 37,000,000 hectares of land that may be considered cultivable. This does not include irrigable land that may amount to an additional several hundred thousand hectares. The potentially cultivable land, still excluding irrigable land, makes about 39% of the total area of the country. Of this potentially arable land only about 18% is at present under cultivation.

It appears, therefore, that the country has still a tremendous reserve of land resources. But we must remember that deforestation, farming malpractices, and mismanagement for centuries have left only an impoverished and exhausted soil.[3] At present, less than 5% of the total area of the country is under forest. Even this very small proportion of forest cover, which is fast diminishing, is a result of inaccessibility rather than of conservation. Over much of northern Ethiopia, strands of trees are seen only around settlements and urban centres as well as in church compounds. Most of the land is absolutely treeless, so much so that in some rural areas only stones are used for building houses, and cow dung for fuel. Wood, even for ploughs and other implements, is very scarce, and farmers have to walk long distances into the more remote valleys to get it.

Deforestation, cultivation of steep slopes and centuries of mismanagement, together with the rugged configuration and torrential rainfall, have caused serious erosion. If one flies low over northern Ethiopia one will easily observe the unmistakable evidence of erosion. In many parts of the northern half of the country, the marks of the ploughshare, of the farm outline, and of the round houses can be seen on the bedrock. Erosion has certainly played havoc with the country's most important resource, the soil.[4]

Although the impoverishment and even total removal of the soil reduces the estimated reserve of the cultivable land, there is still much land that can be utilized. With greater care and more scientific management, the agricultural potential of the country is still high, if the problem of rainfall variability can be overcome by water conservation schemes and by developing new drought-resistant seeds.

About 41% of the country receives an annual rainfall of less than 800 mm, which is considered to be the minimum for crop production in the relatively hot areas. But it is the variation rather than the total yearly rainfall that is problematic, because peasants have no way of adjusting themselves to the fluctuations. In much of the Southeastern Lowlands, the Awash Valley, the Afar Depression, the Coastal Plains and the Barka Lowlands in the north as well as in the lowlands along the Sudanese border, the coefficient of variation for the annual rainfall is in excess of 40%. More than half of the country has over 30% variation. As may be expected, the highest fluctu-

ations occur in regions of marginal rainfall. The coefficient of variation for the seasonal rainfalls is even higher. The probability of four
or five years out of twenty having less than 800 mm of annual rainfall is high in the whole country except the western part.

The Socio-economic Condition of Peasant Life

A. *Land: The Basis of Life.* The life of the Ethiopian peasant is
very closely tied to the land, which is the only source of life and
subsistence in rural Ethiopia. Almost the only avenue open to the
peasant, and almost the only way of making a living in rural Ethiopia, is by tilling the land. The size of cultivable land that the peasant
possesses or has at his disposal, the availability of grazing land nearby, and the number of pairs of oxen that he can muster to plough
his fields, together with the generosity of nature, or, as he himself
would put it, the will of God, determine his level of life.

For the Ethiopian peasant in the past, land was as invaluable as
life itself. Consequently, land is outside the realm of commerce.
Land for the Ethiopian peasant is not a commodity that could be
bought or sold.[5]

Basically, there were only two ways of acquiring land in traditional
rural Ethiopia: one was through inheritance, and the other
through a government grant. Land was considered to be the birthright of every human being, the term human being, or *yesew lij*,
being narrowly defined to exclude artisans. This latter group, because
they were considered subhuman, did not have the right to possess
land.[6] In some parts of Ethiopia, sex and religion were also a basis
for exclusion, women and Muslims being disallowed the possession
of land, but this was the exception rather than the rule.

Land was not only the basis of life or the fountain of life in the
material sense, but, more importantly, in the social and psychological sense as well. Socially, land was the only material evidence for
the claim of *yesew lij*, respectability, and ultimately for the identity
of the individual and his membership to a community. Without
land, no matter how small the size nor how impoverished and useless the quality, the individual lost identity, respectability, and without any material basis he would have no social or communal roots.
Such a condition denies the landless individual the ordinary human
rights, and reduces him to a subhuman status.

This material, social and psychological bond between the peasant and the land was so strong that the peasant generally remained

in his village community until death. To detach himself from the land, which was the source of all his rights as a respectable human being, would require an absolutely certain guarantee not only for his continued sustenance but also for his respectability. This guarantee often came when peasants became rifle-carrying attendants of some *Ras* or *Dejazmach*.[7] In such cases, the rifle provided the means of extorting his provision from peasants, and the servile association with the *Ras* or *Dejazmach* or some dignitary gave him some aura of respectability. By and large, the Ethiopian peasant remained fixed to his land, the land of his ancestors and the land that would pass to those offspring who survived him.

It is not necessary here to discuss the genesis of absolute private ownership of land. It is sufficient to mention that this development was initiated by the Italian invasion and the consequent disruption of the traditional system and values. Other factors that contributed to it are the introduction of cash crops, the development of commercial farms, the deliberate confusion of the traditional *ghebbar*[8] system with private ownership, and the gradual transformation of landowning peasants into tenants, and their gradual eviction. The expropriated peasants are first turned into tenants, then evicted, and eventually turned into agricultural proletarians. This process of alienation was fundamentally opposed to the traditional system that was based on communal landownership. As mentioned above, in traditional rural Ethiopia the majority of the people owned land; it was only the artisans everywhere, and women and Muslims in some parts of Ethiopia, who were denied this right. The more recent development followed and enlarged that traditional pattern to create two classes of citizens, based on right to land. What is important to understand in this connection is that the expropriation of the peasants, on one hand, and the concentration of land ownership in the hands of relatively few individuals, on the other, introduced a tremendous economic gap between the rulers and the ruled. This gap did not exist in traditional Ethiopia (See *Figure 3*).

B. *Subsistence Production.* We have already identified five characteristics of subsistence production. It remains to show now whether, in accordance with these five characteristics, the majority of the Ethiopian peasant fall under a subsistence production system.

Small and fragmented holdings, the first characteristic features of subsistence production, are easily demonstrable in the case of Ethiopian peasant farming. According to the Second Round Rural

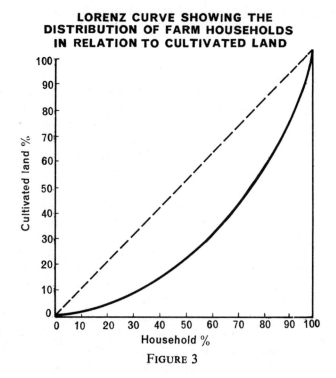

FIGURE 3

Survey of the Central Statistical Office, 2.4% of the peasant holdings are 2,000 square metres (0.2 ha.) or less; 5.3% are 3000 square
metres or less; and almost 70% of the holdings are 4 hectares or
less.[9] But about 7.7% of the farm households own more than 30%
of the cultivated land, as is shown in *Table VII*.

TABLE VII

FARM HOUSEHOLDS AND CULTIVATED LAND BY SIZE OF FARMS,
CUMULATIVE % 1968-1970

	Category of Farm Size, Hectares								
	<4.0	<3.0	<2.0	<1.0	<0.5	<0.2	<0.1	<0.05	Total
Hhs. Cum. %	7.7	11.1	17.8	38.2	64.1	88.3	95.6	98.5	100.0
Land Cum, %	30.1	37.2	47.8	69.4	87.1	97.6	99.5	99.9	100.0

Hhs.—Households; Cum.—Cumulative
Source: Central Statistical Office.

The average holding of 63 farms in two villages, Galmo and Terre near Alemaya, in Harerghe, was found to be 1.5 hectares. The size of holdings ranged "from 0.07 (700 square metres) to 5.6 hectares."[10]

The 63 farms were grouped into size classifications based on increments of 0.50 hectares. Each size group had one or more farms, except that from 4.50-4.99 which had no observations. The largest number of observations, twenty, was in the 0.50-0.99 size group. Twenty-six of the farms had less than one hectare. Forty-nine of the 63 farms had less than two hectares.[11]

These farms are fragmented into small plots that are used for different single crops, or combinations of crops, the average number of plots being four.[12]

In another study made of 59 farms, the average size of cultivated holdings was 2.05 hectares, and the average number of fragments was 3.4.[13] Another group of 60 farms had an average size of 1.93 hectares, and the average number of fragments was three.[14]

The second characteristic feature of subsistence production is the primitive tools and implements that the peasants use.[15] Perhaps the best way of expressing the worth of these tools and implements may be in terms of their money value. The average "estimated inventory value of hand tools and farm equipment" per farm was 30.58 Birr, ranging from 7.50 to 69.00 Birr.[16] In fact this value is much higher than other studies indicate; for instance, in Arsi, the value ranges from 4.25 to 14.00 Birr only.[17] In the face of these facts, it will not be difficult to imagine how primitive these tools and implements are. Working under such oppressive poverty and ignorance, the use of chemical fertilizers is practically unknown to most peasants. Even in Shewa, where one would expect the influence of Addis Ababa to be salubrious and where facilities of marketing are relatively better, in 45 different villages studied by senior geography students, only 3% of the peasants used chemical fertilizers.[18]

What may be surprising is the low labour input on peasant farms (Figure 4a and Figure 4b). The studies made by the senior geography students indicate a labour input of mean man-days ranging from about 22 to about 60 per hectare.[19] Lars Leander, in his study of the two villages in Chilalo, gives figures ranging from 252 man-hours to 971 man-hours per hectare per year.[20] Another study of relatively big farm in Arsi gives the average man-hours per hectare as 267.[21] Generally there is a very clear inverse relationship between farm size and labour input, the smaller the farm size, the higher the labour input. From the studies made by the geography students, there does not seem a clear and definite relationship between labour input and revenue.

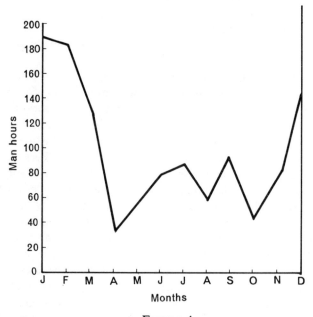

MONTHLY DISTRIBUTION OF LABOUR FOR CROP PRODUCTION AS % DEVIATION MAN-HOURS DIGELU, 1967

FIGURE 4a

The third characteristic feature of subsistence production is the kind of crops and the amount of production. We recognize that, under conditions of subsistence production, peasants work to satisfy their basic need for food. Consequently, the production of grains and pulses becomes their principal preoccupation. What kind of grains and pulses they produce depends on the climatic and soil conditions.

Coming to the 63 farms cited earlier, we find that slightly more tham 85% of the cultivated land was devoted to food production.[22] Actually, on a national scale, according to the Second Round Rural

**MONTHLY DISTRIBUTION OF
OXEN LABOUR AS % OF
DEVIATION FROM MONTHLY
MEAN OX-PAIR DAYS DIGELU, 1967**

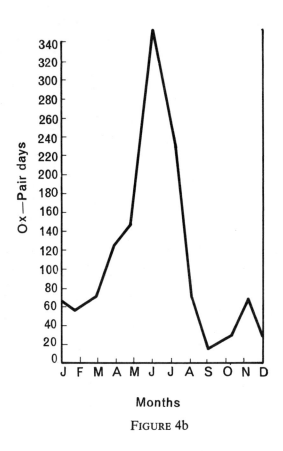

Months

FIGURE 4b

Survey of the Central Statistical Office (CSO), the cultivated land under food crops, including pulses and *inset*, accounts for almost 94% of the total.[23] The major food crops are *tef* (*Eragrostis tef*), wheat, barley, *dagussa* (*Eleusine corocana* : Millet) maize, sorghum, *inset*, and pulses. *Tef* occupies nearly 22% of the total cultivated land, followed by barley, with 16%, sorghum with nearly 15%, maize 14%, and wheat 8%. Pulses alone account for about 12%. The most dominant cash crop of the country, coffee, occupies only 3% of the "cultivated" land.[24]

In the study of ten farms in Digelu and Yeloma, Chilalo, there were three farmers who had more than 50% of their cultivated land under flax, which is a cash crop, while three other farmers had 100% of their cultivated land under food crops. Of the remaining four farmers one had 96%, one 90% another 73%, and the last one 96% of cultivated land under food crops.[25] And these farmers were in a unique area where millions of dollars had been spent by the Swedish government for agricultural development.

In a survey made of some fourteen *weredas* or districts from 87 to 98% of the peasants described their occupation as food production.[26] The most interesting and, perhaps, revealing as well as instructive aspect of their condition, however, lies in their assessment of food production as an occupation: in all the *weredas*, from 94 to 100%, of the peasants believed that "the most respected occupation in the community" was food production. For a people who know hunger, for a people who are too familiar with the gnawing pain of famine, surely, food production is the most respected occupation. But it is important to grasp the full import of the peasants' high value of food production as an occupation: it means, amongst other things, that the basic and nagging need for food has possessed the vast majority of the peasants so much that they are arrested by it, trapped in it, with no better alternative than to make the best of their situation and struggle for survival.

And struggle for survival is the other name of their risky occupation. Famine being the intermittent result of the subsistence production sub-system, undernourishment and malnutrition are a common characteristic of Ethiopian rural life. In the survey made by the Development Through Cooperation Campaign, an average of 68% of the peasants stated that food deficit was normal. With respect to the twelve months preceding the survey, an average of 64% of the peasants interviewed stated that they exprienced food deficit.[27] The survey made by the Central Statistical Office indicates that 83 *weredas* are deficient in *tef*, 43 in wheat, 54 in barley, 45 in sorghum, 58 in maize, 7 in millet, and 69 in pulses.[28] Coming back to the ten farms in Arsi, on the basis of 210 kgs per person per year, three farmers were grossly in deficit, two are below the requirement, two were only slightly above the requirement. When deductions are made for taxes, rent, and seeds, more farmers fall below the requirement.[29] By the same reckoning, only three farmers out of 63 are able to meet more than their yearly requirement in Terre and Galmo villages.[30]

These facts inevitably lead us to the conclusion that a very large proportion of the peasants are hardly able to produce food for themselves and their families. A number of studies have been made by the staff of the Ethiopian Nutrition Institute. One of them comes to the following conclusion:

> In the dietary studies . . . special interest was paid to to the age group $\frac{1}{2}$—3 years of age. It was found that the calorie intake for this age group in all 5 years under study was below, often much below the minimum requirements.[31]

Another study states that a "grossly deficient diet was found in 30 per cent or more of the toddlers with respect to calories, protein, calcium, vitamin A, thiamin, riboflavin, niacin and ascorbic acid."[32] The conclusions reached by other studies are similar.[33] In this respect the Ethiopian Nutrition Institute has made a substantial contribution, for a number of dietary studies have been conducted in various parts of the country. These studies reiterate the problem of food in rural Ethiopia.

At the best, the Ethiopian rural population satisfies its minimal subsistence needs for only about six to nine months of the year. The remaining three to six months is a yearly phenomenon of seasonal hunger, or the so-called pre-harvest hunger. A dietary study made in the Rift Valley of Ethiopia states:

> At the end of the dry season the yield of milk becomes low because of poor pasture. The main crop, corn, is nearly finished and, as a result the food available for consumption in the families investigated was quite insufficient at the time. Thus, there is an ample supply of cereals and a relatively large production of milk in one season whereas in another, most food items are scarce.[34]

In more precise terms:

> In the hungry season the adequacy of calories was on the 55
> per cent level, while during the harvest season it was close to 100
> per cent. The protein intake rose from 80 per cent of the recom-
> mended value during the hungry season to well above 100 per cent
> during the harvest season.[35]

Although this regular period of hunger is general in rural Ethiopia,
its length and seriousness vary from region to region, depending, to
some extent on the quality of the physical environment.

This fact of seasonal hunger that occurs every year in rural
Ethiopia is concrete evidence for the proposition that, taking the
year as a whole, the majority of people of rural Ethiopia live at a
level that is below subsistence. The normally low level of nourishment coupled with the pre-harvest hunger indicate, it must be
observed, not only the level of consumption, but the level of
production as well.

We have been emphasizing the very obvious in order to make the
points that Ethiopian peasants do not in the first place produce for
the market and in the second place do not have surplus to take the
market. Basically most peasants have hardly any need for cash, and
whenever that need does make itself felt, it is externally imposed, as
we shall see later.

The study of the sixty-three farms already referred to earlier
shows that only 7% of the sorghum production, 2% of the maize,
and 22% of the *tef* was sold. Even of the so-called cash crops, the
most important being *chat* (*Catha edulis*) only 31% of the total
production reached the market. In terms of proportion the most
important market crops were hot pepper (90%), onions (75%), Irish
potatoes (50%), and sweet potatoes (21%), the latter having even
lesser proportion than *chat*.[36] But these crops occupy only an
insignificant proportion of the cultivated land, and the production
in absolute terms is rather small. The total amount sold from all
the 63 farms had a value of 6,178,5 Birr, or an average of 98.07
Birr per farm. If what they sell is so low, what they buy is even
less. What do they buy? "The largest item of expense for the
group as a whole was for food, which amounted to 45 per cent for
all farms."[37] The writer concludes, "Even the largest farms, those
with two or more hectares, are at a very low subsistence level."[38]

The expenditures for food appear to contradict the assumption that these are self-sufficing farms. However, these expenditures for food were met by weekly and often daily sales of farm products exchanged in the local market for the kinds of products which the farms in this area were not producing during certain seasons.[39]

Eighty-one members of the 63 farms spent a total of 169.5 man-days per week, or about 2.10 man-days each, for market trips.[40] This may give the very wrong impression that these peasants are very much market-oriented and that there is a large volume of commercial transaction. Nothing can be further from the truth. To demonstrate the special circumstances of the peasants and the peculiar function of the market, we will consider the result of another study of only three farms. Members of three farms spent a total of 3,889 hours on various farm work, and 1,755 hours for the journeying to and from market.[41] The annual cash receipts for the three farms amounted to 870-75 Birr, or an average of 290.25 Birr per farm. For the three farms, the total cash expenditure in the market was 110,75 Birr, amounting to 0.06 per hour spent in the market. All the three farmers bought a considerable proportion of their food. Each of the three farmers bought respectively, 26.7%, 54.3%, and 63.7%, of the total basic food crops they consumed.[42]

Coming back to the numerous market trips made by the farmers, we find that one farmer had a cash income of 500,35 Birr from the sale of farm products in 81 days during the year; another one sold his produce on 180 different days to get 155.25 Birr. Ultimately, when the balance between cash income and cash expenses for the year is made, only one farmer out of the three comes out with a surplus of 47.95 Birr; the remaining two end the year with a deficit of 1.50 and 79.45 respectively.[43] It must be noted that these are peasants who are fortunate enough to have the College of Agriculture in their vicinity. The details of these numerous market trips are evident in *Table VIII*.

Rural people do not go to the market for commercial transaction alone. The market has other even more important social functions for the rural people who live in highly scattered and isolated dwellings. The market provides an occasion and opportunity for social interaction on a wider scale, as well as a form of recreation

TABLE VIII
ANNUAL CASH FAMILY LIVING EXPENSES
JULY 1963-JULY 1964

Item	Number of Annual Market Trips and Total Expenses					
	Family A		Family B		Family C	
	No.	Birr	No.	Birr	No.	Birr
Clothing	7	47.05	3	7.10	3	36.50
Contributions	21	82.00	13	15.20	19	22.50
Sorghum	1	1.30	68	40.50	97	69.85
Corn	1	44.00	29	11.85	36	17.85
Teff	1	26.00	9	4.50	10	3.55
Wheat	2	2.50	5	2.05	—	—
Barley	1	0.25	9	3.80	—	—
Beans	—	—	112	1.25	3	1.20
Peas	3	0.45	16	1.75	8	0.80
Flax	5	0.25	—	—	4	0.35
Meat	11	33.50	3	3.10	—	—
Butter	4	1.85	13	1.40	1	0.25
Milk	6	3.20	6	3.10	2	0.10
Coffee hulls	21	2.30	46	2.45	49	2.65
Tobacco	11	1.15	49	2.75	223	11.15
Chat	—	—	—	—	1	5.00
Fenugreek	29	2.55	30	1.50	70	3.50
Pepper	40	2.00	18	0.90	5	0.25
Salt	84	8.25	52	2.60	150	9.50
Kerosene	87	6.65	96	3.40	143	9.25
Hair oil	4	0.50	31	1.95	58	3.00
Incense	9	0.45	4	0.20	15	0.75
Laundry soap	12	1.30	1	0.05	20	2.15
Spaghetti	5	0.85	—	—	—	—
Grain-grinding	11	1.25	—	—	2	0.25
Medicine	2	2.25	1	0.75	2	6.00
Transportation	1	1.50	—	—	2	2.00
Cooking oil	7	1.55	—	—	10	2.25
Miscellaneous	—	3.20	—	4.90	—	9.45
Total		277.85		117.03		220.00

Source: Leonard F. Miller and Telehum Makonnen, *op. cit.*, p. 43.

and temporary relief from rural boredom.[44]

The proper marketing function is limited by various factors. In the first place, the scale and method of individual farm production is so severely constrained that output significantly exceeding consumption requirements is rare. In the second place, the scarcity of cash limits the volume of transaction, often reducing it to cents rather than dollars. In fact, in some remote rural areas, paper money is not accepted as currency at all. In some markets only the fifty-cent silver coin or the ten-cent coin are the means of exchange. In the third place, along the borders of the country, anarchy in currency limits commercial transaction. In these peripheral areas the currencies of the neighbouring countries are more in demand than Ethiopian money.

The point that must be stressed is that, although some agricultural products of peasants reach the market, they are insignificant both in volume and value. The more important point, however, is the fact that the production of the peasants is not influenced by the market. It is need and habit that govern the production of the peasants.[45] When the farmer plans his production he does not calculate either the input or the final output in terms of cash, nor does he proceed to use available resources for maximum returns.[46]

It was stated earlier that the need for cash is externally imposed on the peasants. Traditionally peasants paid their dues to whoever had a claim in terms of their produce and labour. This was slowly changed into cash obligations for taxes, rent, and other extortions. For the three farms cited earlier, the total annual income was 870.75 Birr (550.35 Birr being the share of one farmer), of which 146.1 Birr was paid out in form of tax, rent, and fine.[47] For the 63 farms, land "taxes averaged 27 per cent of all farm expenses."[48] In Digelu, the total cash income from the sale of field crops was 303.05 Birr for the five farmers, who together paid a total of 247.40 Birr in taxes and rents.[49] By contrast, the Yeloma farmers were far better off. The bureaucratic indifference to the suffering of famine victims is demonstrated by the fact that, in 1973, at the time of the devastating famine in Wello, peasants were required to pay their tax obligations, shown in *Table IX*.

An equally important point that we must bear in mind is the fact that, if and when the peasants' produce reaches the market in whatever size or form, the peasants are not really engaged in a voluntary transaction on their own behalf and to promote their own interest. They go to the market mainly because they are forced to exchange their produce for cash which they need to meet their various obligations. Viewed in this context, the market becomes a very crucial element of the socio-economic and political

TABLE IX
TAX ESTIMATES BY *Awraja* FOR WELLO, 1973,
in 1,000 birr

Awraja Name	1	2	3	4	5	6	7	8	9	Total
Borena	76.6	9.9	66.9	66.9	9.2	210.0	31.3		1.7	472.6
Werre-Himeno	103.2	1.2	52.1	52.1	0.7	156.3	28.8		0.2	403.6
Wadla-Delanta	45.1	0.1	23.1	23.1	2.1	63.2	5.8			162.5
Wag	23.5	11.7	37.4	37.4	3.9	133.8	20.5		0.7	268.9
Lasta	12.2	2.7	27.2	37.2	0.1	136.8	0.9		0.0	207.1
Yeju	75.0	3.3	38.9	38.9	5.9	113.9	23.8		0.5	300.8
Ambassel	195.1	19.5	102.8	102.8	12.4	226.6	30.6	1.1	0.5	690.3
Awsa	54.6	10.2	31.6	31.6	0.2	76.6	0.4	0.0		233.0
Qallu	90.1	3.8	48.4	48.4	4.0	111.7	11.0	27.8	0.2	317.6
Grand Total	675.4	62.4	428.4	428.4	47.5	1228.9	152.6	28.9	3.8	3056.3

1. Land tax
2. Tithe
3. Education tax
4. Health tax
5. Church health tax

6. Agricultural income tax
7. Church agricultural income tax
8. Livestock tax (for nomads)
9. Church tithe

Source: Ministry to Interior.

sub-system and a very potent instrument of exploitation rather than a means of voluntary interaction.

The need for cash imposed on the peasants is only the tail end of a need that commences far beyond the borders of the country. The imperialist need for economic domination titillates and corrupts the ruling class and the bourgeoisie in order to create in them the need for consumer goods. The ruling class and the bourgeoisie, in turn, armed with their imperialist appetite for conspicuous consumption and with corporate power, find the peasants a very easy prey, a very stable, although a very modest, source of cash. As a result, the peasants may starve with their wives and children, while their need for cash becomes a more pressing and a more powerful force than hunger. Whatever cash need the peasants may have, therefore, is first and foremost to pay their obligations to the government, the landlords, and the maladministrators. From the results of the surveys made by senior geography students, the following conclusion was reached:

The index of monetization for more than 80 per cent of the households surveyed is less than 0.20. This means that less than 20 per cent of the total produce of each farm family is sold in the market. For the remaining some 20 per cent of the farm households the rate of monetization ranges from 20 to 50 per cent on the average.[50]

Since the total production of the peasants is very often insufficient to meet even their subsistence needs, these external demands for cash aggravate their already abysmally poor conditions of living.

This brings us to the fourth characteristic feature of subsistence production, lack of seasonal employment opportunities. For the peasants, there is almost no possibility of augmenting their farm income by some seasonal employment in the nearby towns. The rural areas themselves, of course, have no such seasonal employment facilities. According to the second round of the survey made by the Central Statistical Office, in the 82 *awrajas* included in the survey, there were only a total of 109,600 employers and 319,100 employees.[51] Most of those who need labour have many ways of getting it free. Subtle pressure, patronage, or the "favour" of lending a few kilograms of grain at high interest are some of the ways. In some parts of the country, the peasants pay the interest

for money or grain they borrow in the form of labour by working
a given number of days a week for the lender. But even this opportunity, if opportunity it can be called, of harsh exploitation is very
limited. In the rural areas of Ethiopia, the average wage that an
employee gets is 15 to 25 Birr per annum plus some meagre food.

The foregoing discussion leads us to the inescapable conclusion
that more than 81% of Ethiopian peasants live under abject
poverty, not relative but absolute poverty.[52] That they starve three
to six months every year when natural conditions are said to be
normal, that they periodically sink from their precarious subsistence level into the abyss of famine, and that they are unable to
sell their labour seasonally for some cash or grain are not exceptional but regular conditions of existence. Especially during the
critical "hungry season", the daily affirmation of their penury and
helplessness in the face of the humiliating misery and suffering of
their wives and children drives them into debt.[53]

Debt is the inevitable result of rural penury. Without any reserves
of grain or cash, the fifth characteristic of subsistence production,
the vast majority of the rural population were forced into debt when
they reach the brink of starvation. Rural Ethiopia had become a
fertile ground for people who had some cash reserves, to double or
even quadruple it in less than a year. Lending money, or grain, at
extortionate rates of interest that might often reach 200% or more
a year was becoming a very lucrative business. There were other
ways by which the rich farmers and rural merchants exploited the
hardship of the peasants. Two or three months before the harvest,
when the peasants were at their worst time, the rural merchants
"bought" the unharvested grain at ridiculously low prices. Ultimately, for the peasants, there was very little difference whether
they borrowed cash at exorbitantly high interest or "sold" their
expected harvest. Even if this did not happen, excess supply at harvest time would bring prices plummeting so low that they would be
forced to sell more of their produce in order to meet their obligations. Even under better economic conditions, as Galbraith remarks
in "both the markets in which he sells and those in which he buys,
the individual farmer's market power in the typical case is intrinsically nil".[54]

Ethiopian peasants were under the burden of deadweight debt
from year to year. A rough estimate from the survey of the Central
Statistical Office appears to suggest that the peasants carried a debt

TABLE X

PERCENTAGE OF NUMBER OF LOANS BY TENANCY OF RECIPIENT
HOUSEHOLDS AND BY SOURCE OF LOAN 1968-1971

Source of Loan	Percentage of Number of Loans by Tenancy of Recipient Households				Tota
	Owners Only	Tenants Only	Owner Tenants	Not stated	
Own landlord	0.0	81.2	8.9	9.9	100.0
Trader	37.6	38.3	10.4	13.7	100.0
Landowner	41.2	32.8	12.6	13.3	100.0·
Church	62.0	9.8	16.3	11.8	100.0
Bank	91.3	8.7	0 0	0.0	100.0
Others	30.2	46.0	11.5	12.3	100.0
Not stated	32.5	44.7	8.0	14.8	1C0.0
Average	42.1	37.4	9.7	10.8	100.0

Source: Based on data from the Central Statistical Office.

TABLE XI

PERCENTAGE OF NUMBER OF LOANS BY TENANCY OF RECIPIENTS
AND PURPOSE OF LOAN, 1968-1971

Purpose	Tenancy of Recipients				Total
	Owner Only	Tenants Only	Owner Tenants	Not Stated	
Food	32.2	41.5	11.4	14.9	100.0
Clothing	40.4	38.6	10.3	10.6	100.0
Medical	37.5	45.2	5.5	11.8	100.0
Building	45.3	31.0	14.7	8.9	100.0
Ceremonies	39.4	42.0	8.1	10.4	100.0
Taxes	47.8	32.7	8.8	10.7	100.0
Investment	31.8	40.6	20.3	9.7	100.0
Trading	31.0	34.6	13.6	20.8	100.0
Other	34.8	38.9	12.7	13.5	100.0
Not stated	31.7	37.7	13.6	17.0	100.0
Average	37.1	38.2	11.9	12.8	100.0

Source: Based on data from the Central Statistical Office.

amounting to almost 55 million Birr.[55] Slightly more than 47% of
the indebted peasants owed up to 20 Birr, about 35.5% owed 20 to
60 Birr, and only slightly more than 4% of them owed more than

150 Birr. Confirming desirability of debt-worthiness, about 40% of
the indebted peasants were landowning peasants, 32% were tenants,
and 19% were partly owners and partly tenants.[56] The most important single purpose of these loans was for purchasing food which
accounted for 48% of the total number of loans in the *awrajas*
surveyed.

We may now be in a position to understand the subsistence production system in more concrete terms. Under a subsistence phoduc-
tion system, the obligations of the peasants to outsiders have priority over their own needs. They are forced to sell their produce to
meet their cash obligations. By a different set of conditions they are
all forced to sell at about the same time as harvest time. Coming out
of the pre-harvest hungry season, prodded by lenders and tax collec-
tors, the peasants are in no position to withhold their produce from
the market until they can command better prices. The only alternative they have is selling more at low prices. This may illuminate our
conception of the subsistence production system in which the socio-
economic and political forces, as well as the more or less simultaneous harvest seasons, conspire against the peasants to invalidate the
often repeated statement that was reiterated earlier: In a subsistence
economy, production equals consumption. The fact is, as we have
seen,

$$P = T + D + C \text{ and, therefore}$$
$$C = P - (T + D),$$

where P stands for production, T for taxes, D for debts, and C for
consumption. In other words tax and other obligations and debts
have a definite priority over consumption. The peasants may be said
to be outside subsistence production, when

$$P = T + D + C + S,$$

where S stands for surplus.

In the absence of some surplus after obligations and consumption
are deducted from production, we can only talk of subsistence production. Even those peasants who are now accustomed to the production of cash crops have hardly raised themselves beyond the
subsistence level, although their participation in commercial intercourse has certainly enlarged their capacity to gain cash. Raanan

Weitz remarked, "An indiscriminate introduction of cash crops has often resulted in the substitution of subsistence living for subsistence production."[57] His distinction between subsistence living (if the phrase is not tautological) and subsistence production is helpful, in that it identifies those peasants who are just beginning to commercialize their production as a separate transitional group. But his statement that "their existence is more precarious than that of traditional subsistence farmers, as the risks of the market fluctuations are added to the vagaries of nature"[58] appears to be only a theoretical assumption. Price fluctuations are only an occasional and admittedly negative aspect of the market. But we cannot, at the same time, ignore the compensating mechanism in the fluctuations themselves, as well as the many positive lessons of the market, such as economy, foresight, and the risks and rewards of commerce.

Weitz, however, identifies subsistence production in very precise terms. He characterizes subsistence production as follows:

> In the traditional subsistence farming, output and consumption are almost identical, and the staple crop—usually wheat, barley, sorghum, rice, or corn—is the chief source of caloric intake. Output and productivity are low and tools are simple. Capital investment is negligible, while land and labour are the key production factors. Labour is underutilized; workers are largely idle during the rest of the year. Requirements at peak seasons determine the upper limit of the size of individual farms. The peasant cultivates only as much land as his family is able to work without recourse to hired labour. Agriculture is still in this stage in much of the underdeveloped world, and will continue to be as long as the environment remains static.[59]

On this, one must strongly agree with him. But, then, Weitz presents "diversification or mixed farming" as a "breakthrough"[60] out of subsistence production. The former is distinguished from the latter by livestock raising, which "constitutes an integral part of the production system", and by "a sizeable share of the produce" being "destined" for the market.[61] There does not seem to be any necessary connection between diversification or mixed farming, on one hand, and commercialization, on the other. In Ethiopia, both livestock raising and diversification of crop production are common features of subsistence production. Theoretically it is, perhaps, correct to raise diversified or mixed farming to a higher category than farms engaged in the production of one or two food crops, for the former suggests an enlarged production capacity with which surplus production is assumed. This assumption, however, ignores "the irreducible claims of outsiders" that keeps the peasants at subsistence level.

In Ethiopia, diversification is one of the most cardinal features, as well as one of the manifestations of the inefficiency of subsistence production: witness *Table XII*. Under Ethiopian subsistence production, diversification serves three purposes. It is, first, a means of protecting the peasants from natural risks and total loss, for they know one or two crops may be relatively more resistant to drought or diseases. Second, diversification enables the peasants to have some crops that may be consumed green, and therefore serve to alleviate the scarcity of food during the pre-harvest "hungry season." Third, diversification, as a deliberate production mechanism that eschews the market, allows the peasants to have a variety of complementary foodstuffs that will enhance their feeling of self-sufficiency, or a measure of independence from the market.[62] In fact diversification is one of the principal characteristics of Ethiopian subsistence production, while at the same time it is an explicit manifestation of its weakness and vulnerability, a result of uncertainty and fear.

Scott is right in identifying the "safety-first"[63] principle as underlying purpose of subsistence production. Insofar as the activities of peasants are almost totally oriented to meeting their basic subsistence needs, their production pattern may be rationalized by a "safety-first" principle, provided we remain within the peasant world. But the problem is that Scott builds his principle on an economic rationalization that is alien to peasants. "In the choice of seeds and techniques of cultivation," Scott writes, "[Safety first] means simply that *the cultivator prefers to minimize the probability of having a disaster rather than maximizing his average return*" (emphasis added).[64] Scott does recognize the problem: "A critical assumption of the safety first rule is that subsistence routines are producing satisfactory results. What if they are not? Here the rationale of safety-first breaks down."[65] The idea of choice is so deeply ingrained in Western thought that no necessary activity can be contemplated without it. If choice implies available alternatives for selecting better seeds, better techniques, and other possibilities for

TABLE XII
LAND UTILIZATION BY FARMERS A, B AND C, JULY 1962

	Farmer A		Farmer B		Fārmer C	
	Size ha.	%	Size ha.	%	Size ha.	%
Single Cropping						
Chat	0.55	12.94	..	..	0.17	13.49
Barley	..	..	0.06	4.69	..	..
Teff	0.18	4.24	0.05	3.90	0.05	3.97
Wheat	0.14	3.29	..	..	..	..
Sorghum	0.26	6.12	..	..	..	..
Fenugreek	..	..	..	..	0.02	1.59
Lentils	..	..	..	..	0.03	2.38
Flax	0.01	0.24	..	..	..	..
Corn	0.01	0.24	..	..	..	..
Sweet potatoes	0.02	0.47	0.08	6.25	0.09	7.14
Mixed Cropping						
Chat and Beans	0.04	0.9ᵽ	..	..	..	..
Vegetables	0.25	5.88	..	..	0.04	3.18
Sorghum, Corn, and Beans	..	..	..	..	0.65	51.59
Sweet potatoes, Beans and Corn	..	..	..	..	0.06	4.76
Corn, Beans, Pepper, and Tomatoes	..	..	..	..	0.12	9.52
Chat, Corn, and Fruit Trees	..	..	0.29	22.66	..	..
Sorghum, Potatoes, Corn and Chat	..	..	0.05	3.90	..	..
Sorghum, Corn, Lentils and Beans	9.97	22.82	..	..	..	..
Sorghum, Corn, Beans and Teff	0.09	2,12	..	..	..	..
Corn, Tomatoes, Beans and Sorghum	..	..	0.07	5.47	..	..
Sorghum and Corn	..	..	0.12	9.38	..	..
Free Use of Land by Others	0.24	5.65	..	..	..	..
	2.76	64.95	0.72	56.25	1.23	97.62
Total Cultivated Land						
Sod Land	1.16	27.30	0.30	23.44	..	..
Fallow Land	0.14	3.29	0.24	18.75	..	..
Waste Land	0.14	3.29	..	..	..	..
Courtyard	0.05	1.17	0.02	1.56	0.03	2.38
	1.49	35.05	0.51	43.75	0.03	2.38
Total Non-Cultivated Land						
Total Farm	4.25	100.00	1.28	100.00	1.26	100.00

Note: Farmers A and C had 23 domestic animals between them.
Source: Leonard F. Miller and Tilahun Makonnen.

maximizing returns, then the subsistence producer would be transformed into something else. It is only in despair that they "choose"
to be, in the existentialist sense, subsistence producers and, as has
already been indicated earlier, they even have a tendency to univer-
salize it. If they were to believe that subsistence production is a
lowly and miserable activity, they would lose self-respect.[66]

But as a system, subsistence production is not merely the interaction between peasants, on one hand, and the physical conditions,
on the other. The subsistence production system involves a very
complex interaction between peasants and the physical environment;
between government policies and the physical environment; between
peasants and government; as well as between peasants, on the one
hand, with government officials, traditional and cultural leaders,
landlords and merchants, and sociocultural values on the other. It
is the interaction and the relationship among all these complex
elements of the whole socio-economic fabric of the society that
constitutes what we call the subsistence production system. It is this
system that victimizes the peasants and keeps them in perpetual
poverty.

The Two Risks of Subsistence Production

Insofar as the peasants' productive capacity is concerned, it has
eternally been sandwiched between two risks, one from the natural
sub-system and the other from the socio-economic sub-system. The
peasants perceive the two sub-systems as a unit organized, directed
and controlled by God. Insofar as they are able to identify the elements of the natural sub-system, they perceive them, too, as even
more under the control of God, and therefore outside the realm of
human manipulation. As we have already seen, when the natural
sub-system is favourable and bountiful, then it is an expression of
the mercy and forgiveness of God. Consequently, the reaction of
peasants to the changing conditions of the natural sub-system is
prayer and exhortation, on the one hand, and appreciation and
thanksgiving on the other.

But the peasants do not find such a neat explanation for, nor do
they find a suitable reaction to the socio-economic sub-system.
Baffled by what they call the cruelty of man to man, they tend to
join the socio-economic and the natural sub-systems together and
give them a religious or supernatural explanation. Ultimately, their
role in responding to adverse conditions, whether originating from

the natural or from the socio-economic sub-system, is reduced only to supplicating God as the final arbiter. By and large, the general belief of the peasants exaggerates the role of God and diminishes their own. At the same time, the peasants do vaguely recognize the distinction between the risk emanating from the natural sub-system and the one originating from the socio-economic one.

The risk that peasants confront from the natural sub-system is basically different. An unexpected condition of nature destroys or substantially reduces their expected harvest or production. In this case they lose what they laboured for, but they lose what they did not get. They lose only what they expected. As a result, the risk that originates from the natural sub-system easily lends itself to supernatural intervention and acquires a bearable quality. This is not so with the risk engendered by the socio-economic sub-system. In this case, the peasants face the risk of losing what they have actually produced, what is already in their hands. This makes it an enervating and an unbearable risk. Moreover, it is more persistent than the risk from the natural sub-system which takes place only occasionally.

The occasional risk from the natural sub-system is in fact a risk only because the subsistence production system under which the peasants struggle for existence is vulnerable. By unmitigated and constant exploitation, by substantially reducing the production of the peasants and thereby rendering them deficient of any reserves, and forcing them into a marginal life, the socio-economic sub-system creates vulnerability. Because of this vulnerability, and slight change in the expected condition of physical environment sharply increases the risk of famine.

So conceived, subsistence production system is self-impoverishing. By impoverishing the peasants and keeping them perpetually at a low level of subsistence, the system ensures the conspicuous consumption of a small minority and the degradation of the vast majority. The minority that is superimposed on the majority does not have the necessary social responsibility to appreciate the dismal and vulnerable condition that it has created in the rural areas, nor does it seem to have the ability and the will to anticipate an emergency situation of food shortage. So it is not the peasants alone who are impoverished to a level where they cannot have grain or cash reserves. The whole system of subsistence production lacks any social need for any mechanism of accumulating reserves. That is what is euphemistically called underdevelopment.

NOTES

[1]CSO, *Land Area and Utilization: Results of the National Sample Survey,* (Second Round. Vol. V. Statistical Bulletin 10. Addis Ababa, February 1975).

[2]For the sake of consistency the data used in this study are the results of the CSO's rural survey. The data for cultivated land in the annual Statistical Abstracts are very inconsistent and variable. For instance, the 1971 Statistical Abstract gives the total cultivated land as 10,398,000 ha., while that of 1975 gives only 6,921,000. Although the data from the survey may appear to be gross underestimation, they are more reliable.

[3]See Institute of Agricultural Research, *Progress Report for the Period February 1966 to March 1968* (Addis Ababa, June, 1968), and Roy L. Donahue, *Ethiopia, Taxonomy, Cartography and Ecology of Soils,* Monograph Number 1, Occasional Paper Series (Michigan State University, East Lansing, 1972).

[4]See E.H.F. Swain, *Report to the Government of Ethiopia on Forest Policy and Forest Development* (F.A.O. Report No. 321, Rome December, 1954); W.C. Bosshard, *Report to the Government of Ethiopia on Forest Development,* (F.A.O. Report No. 1143, Rome, 1959).

[5]Since February, 1975, all land in Ethiopia has been nationalized by proclamation. This proclamation is only a modern and legal expression of a traditional concept, although, of course the traditional concept, as already explained, had serious problems of inequality.

[6]See Mesfin Wolde-Mariam, *Introductory Geography of Ethiopia,* (Addis Ababa, 1972), pp. 81-89.

[7]These were traditional titles given by the monarch to rulers of certain regions. They are not hereditary titles.

[8]Mesfin Wolde-Mariam, *Introduction to Geography of Ethiopia, op. cit.,* p. 84.

[9]My own calculation from CSO's *Land Area and Utilization, op. cit.*

[10]K.C. Davis, Ahmed Mohammed, W.A. Wayt, *Farm Organization Terre and Galmo Villages, Harar Province,* (College of Agriculture, Dire Dawa, October, 1965), p. 12.

[11]*Ibid.,* p, 16.

[12]*Ibid.,* p 15.

[13]Demise Gebre Michael, *Land Tenure in Bate, Alemaya Mikitil-Wereda, Harar,* (College of Agriculture, Dire Dawa, June, 1966), p. 29

[14]*Ibid.,* p. 31.

[15]An illustrated description of the peasants' tools and implements is found in the following: eds. and illustrators, Hailu Mengesha, Bob Lee, Haile Yesus Zewge *Domestic Implements of Ethiopia: A Brief Survey of Hand Tools, Household and Farming Implements of Harar Province,* (College of Agriculture, Bulletin No. 5, Dire Dawa, November 1960).

[16]*Farm Organization of Terre and Galmo Villages, op. cit.,* p. 28.

[17]Lars Leander, *A Case Study of Peasant Farmers in Degalu and Yeloma Areas, Chilalo Awraja,* (CADU Publication No. 22, Addis Ababa, January, 1969), p. 20.

[18]Compiled by Girma Kebbede, *Land Use Study in Shewa,* Department of Geography, Addis Ababa University (Mimeographed Copy. Addis Ababa,

August, 1974), p. 24.

[19]*Ibid.*, p. 27.

[20]Lars Leander, *op. cit.*, p. 42.

[21]CADU, *Case Study of Farm Households in the Asella Area*, (CADU Publication No. 78, Addis Ababa. April, 1972), p. 28.

[22]K.C. Davis and others, *op. cit.*, p. 15.

[23]Calculated from data in, *Land Area and Utilization, op. cit.* The CSO data covers only 83 *awrajas*, my own estimates have been included for the remaining 19 *awrajas*.

[24]Peter Koehn argues as do many other writers, that the origin of famine is at least partially traceable to increase in export-oriented crops. He writes, "Many of the large commercial plantations favoured under Haile Selassie's legal order turned fertile lands into the production of non-essential foodstuffs (e.g. sugar) or inedible agricultural commodities destined for export. . ." *op. cit.*, p. 54. Sugarcane occupies a mere 6.900 ha., or 0.13% of the cultivated land. Assumptions that do not correspond to the facts are often misleading, especially when they are repeated by uncritical writers.

[25]Lars Leander, *op. cit.*, p. 38 .

[26]Compiled by Fassil G. Kiros and Assefa Mehretu, data collected by students in Development Through Cooperation Campaign, *Survey of Socioeconomic Characteristics of Rural Ethiopia*, (Institute of Development Research; Addis Ababa. 1975). Research Bulletins 1-14.

[27]*Loc. cit.*

[28]Unpublished *wereda* information acquired from CSO.

[29]Lars Leander, *op. cit.*, p. 49.

[30]K.C. Davis and others. *op. cit.*, pp. 20-23.

[31]M. Belo, K. Jacobsson, G. Tormell, L. Uppsall, B. Laar, B. Vahlquist, "Anthropometric, Clinical and Biochemical Studies in Children from Five Different Regions of Ethiopia", reprinted from, *The Journal of Tropical Pediatrics and Environmental Child Health*, Monograph No. 24 (September, 1972, no pagination. See also Asmerom Kidane. "Incidence of Undernutrition in an Ethiopian Community—A Statistical Study", *Sinet, Eth. J. Sci.*, Vol. I, No. 2.

[32]Ruth Selinus, Abeba Gobezie and Bo Vahlquist, "Dietary Studies in Ethiopia. III. Dietary Pattern Among the Sidamo Ethnic Group", reprinted from *Acta Societatis Medicorum Upsaliensis*. Vol. LXXVI, Nos. 3-4, 1971, p. 171. See also Ruth Selinus, Guenet Awalom and Abeba Gobezie, "Dietary Studies in Ethiopia, II. Dietary Pattern in two Rural Communities in "N. Ethiopia: A Study with Special Attention to the Situation in Young Children", *Acta Societatis Medicorum Upssaliensis*, Vol. LXXVI, Nos. 1-2, 1971.

[33]See, for instance, Mesfin Wolde-Mariam and others, *Welenkomi: A Socioeconomic and Nutritional Survey of a Rural Community in the Central Highlands of Ethiopia*, The World Land Use Survey, Occasional Papers, No. 11 (Tonbridge, 1971).

[34]Ruth Selinus, Abeba Gobezie, K.E. Knutsson and B. Vahlquist, "Dietary Studies in Ethiopia: Dietary Pattern Among the Rift Valley Arsi Galla", reprinted from, *The American Journal of Clinical Nutrition*, 24, March 1971, p. 367.

[35]*Ibid.*, p. 371.

[36]K.C. Davis and others, *op. cit.*, p. 20-24.

[37]*Ibid.*, p. 29.

[38]*Ibid.*, p. 29.

[39]*Ibid.*, p. 29-30.

[40]*Ibid.*, p. 40.

[41]Leonard F. Miller and Telahun Makonnen, *Organization and Operation of Three Ethiopian Case Farms*, (College of Agriculture, Dire Dawa, March, 1965), p. 26.

[42]*Ibid.*, p. 31

[43]*Loc. cit.*

[44]For more detail, see Mesfin Wolde-Mariam, *Introduction to Geography of Ethiopia, op. cit.*, pp. 159-96.

[45]Mesfin Wolde-Mariam, *Cultural Problems of Development, op. cit.*, pp. 5-6.

[46]James C. Scott expresses the idea more convincingly when he says that peasants "living close to the subsistence margin and subject to the vagaries of weather and the claims of outsiders. . . [have] little scope for the profit maximization calculus of traditional neoclassical economics". See James C. Scott, *op. cit.*, p. 4.

[47]Leonard F. Miller and Telahun Makonnen, *op. cit.*, 31

[48]K.C. Davis and others, *op. cit.*, p. 27.

[49]Lars Leander, *op. cit.*, p. 68 and p. 76. See p. 71 and p. 79 for Yeloma.

[50]Girma Kebbede, *op. cit.*, p. 33.

[51]CSO, *The Demography of Ethiopia, op. cit.*, p. 23.

[52]The confusion between relative and absolute poverty leads to the conclusion that there is "no fundamental difference" between developed and underdeveloped countries in so far as the poor in both areas of the world are concerned: Susan George, *op. cit.*, p. 10.

[53]For comparative studies of children, see M. Belo, J. Jacobson, G. Tornell, L. Uppsall, B. Zaar, B. Vahlquist, "Anthropometric, Clinical and Biochemical Studies in Children from Five Different Regions of Ethiopia", reprinted from the *Journal of Tropical Pediatrics and Environmental Child Health,* Monograph No. 24, September, 1972.

[54]John Kenneth Galbraith, *American Capitalism: The Concept of Countervailing Power*, (Penguin London, 1963). p. 168.

[55]CSO, *Indebtedness: Results of the National Sample Survey*, Second Round (Vol. IV, Statistical Bulletin 10. Addis Ababa, August 1974).

[56]*Ibid.*, my own summary calculated from the CSO data.

[57]Raanan Weitz, *From Peasant to Farmer: A Revolutionary Strategy for Development*, (New York, 1971), p. 16.

[58]*Ibid.*, pp. 16-17.

[59]*Ibid.*, p. 16, see also p. 54.

[60]*Ibid.*, p. 17.

[61]*Ibid.*, p. 45.

[62]In Ethiopian tradition selling food was as dishonourable as buying food. One feeds the hungry and to make them pay will be the ultimate meanness. On the other hand there is nothing shameful or in any sense degrading in asking for food in the name of God or some Saint if one is hungry. It is by extending this logic that hungry passers-by could, in traditional Ethiopia, freely help

themselves to green peas, beans, chickpeas or corn from any form without any sense of guilt, and even in the presence of the owner.

[63]James C. Scott, *op. cit.*, pp. 15-26.

[64]*Ibid.,* pp. 17-18.

[65]*Ibid.*, p. 26.

[66]It is interesting to reflect on the rather sharp difference of attitude between Ethiopian and Italian peasants. Unlike the Italian peasant the Ethiopian peasant does not seem to believe that "everything about him is contemptible or ridiculous." See Edward C. Banfield, *The Moral Basis of a Backward Society*, (New York, 1967), pp. 63-66. May be a much closer scrutiny will indicate that Banfield's generalization is true for Ethiopia as well. The Ethiopian peasants may be expressing their defence mechanism rather than their real feeling.

Chapter Five

The Role of the State in Famine

If we accept any one of the theories that attempt to establish the state on idealist philosophical foundations, the Ethiopian state of Emperor Haile Sillase will only serve to falsify it. It certainly did not correspond to Locke's consent of the majority, having as its end "the Mutual Preservation of their Lives, Liberties and Estates,"[1] neither did it correspond to Rousseau's "moral and collective body," or the General Will, having as its end "the preservation and prosperity of its members,"[2] nor did it correspond even to Hobbes's earlier theory that gave everything to the ruler and practically nothing to the ruled, except that he assumed law and order which would be preferable to "miseries and horrible calamities"[3] that might result from anarchy. Definitions of the state derived from these and other similar political theories do not change the fact that the old Ethiopian state did not possess the necessary positive qualities.[4]

In fairness to these political philosophers, it must be said that they were painfully aware of a reality that was quite different from their theoretical prescription. Locke makes a distinction between a King and a Tyrant: "That one makes the Laws and Bounds of his Power, and Good of the Publick, the end of his Government; the other makes all give way to his own Will and Appetite."[5] And Rousseau states, "However little the people gives, if that little does not return to it, it is soon exhausted by giving continually: the State is then never rich, and the people is always a people of beggars." He then comments that "instead of governing subjects to make them happy despotism makes them wretched in order to govern them."[6]

Harold Laski's opening sentence in his *Grammar of Politics* reads: "No theory of the state is ever intelligible save in the context of its time."[7] He then rejects the idealist theories of the state and argues that those who defend them,

> must be able to show not that an ideal state which exists only in their own construction, but the actual states ... that we know, are inherently capable, granted the class-relations they maintain, of fulfilling demand on the largest possible scale, and that, therefore, they have a moral claim to the allegiance of their members on this ground.[8]

In the Ethiopian traditional context, state and government are not separate concepts. The term *menghist* denotes a unified concept of sovereignty and the machinery of power. God is the ultimate source of authority, although it appears that sometimes in certain circumstances the will of God and the will of the people coincide. This notion is expressed in the saying: God's will is the people's will, and the people's will is God's will.[9] This dictum provided a justification for rebellion against a monarch who, although his authority was originally sanctified by holy ointment, was believed to have deviated from the proper exercise of his authority as the trustee of God. It appears that the most important functions of government, in Ethiopian traditional thinking, were the administration of justice and the concern for the welfare of the people. By this standard, too, the old Ethiopian state fell far too short.

Only the Marxist view of the state as an instrument of oppression and exploitation fits the objective conditions in Ethiopia. According to Marx, out of "the contradiction between the interest of the individual and that of the community the latter takes an independent form as the state, divorced from the real interests of individual and community."[10] It is this state and its machinery, representing neither the interest of individuals nor of the community as a whole, but of the ruling class, that we take as an important factor of famine. The recurrent famine situation exposes the utter failure of the state and its machinery if we accept the political theories mentioned earlier, or, alternatively, it confirms the Marxist view.

The part played by the Ethiopian government in famine will now be examined at the levels of information, decision, and action.

Information

There is no doubt that the detail and accuracy as well as the speed and efficiency of processing and transmitting information are crucial, particularly in an impending famine situation. Normally, the original source of information on famine were community leaders. From them, information was transmitted to the lowest administrative sub-division, usually *mikittil wereda*, or *wereda*. If the flow of this information did not encounter any barrier, it would move to *awraja*, *kifle hagher*,[11] Ministry of Interior, the Prime Minister, the Council of Ministers, and, finally, the Emperor. In spite of lack of postal services in many parts of the country and in spite of distance and problems of transport, the flow of information could ideally proceed up through the various levels of administrative hierarchy in a relatively short time, from a few days to about four weeks. But, in practice, the information that might originate from a *mikittil wereda*, or a *wereda*, never flowed smoothly up to the highest level.

There are various reasons for the interruptions in the flow of information. Both the quality and the quantity of information were often defective. Lower-level sources did not specifically identify the problem and assess its magnitude and intensity, nor did they suggest alternative solutions or recommendations. Since most administrators, especially at the lower levels of the hierarchy, were only semi-literate and since they very often had absolutely no facilities of any kind at their disposal, they found it impossible to weigh and confirm any information they received from the people or elders. So they transmitted only what they received. In addition, since these administrators, for the most part, had been appointed to their posts for reasons that had nothing to do with administration and the well-being of the people, and, since the level of their social consciousness was low, they had after only a perfunctory attitude to social problems.

As we go up the administrative echelon, the level of education of at least the junior officials rose, but one cannot unfortunately state that the level of commitment to public welfare rose commensurately. Nevertheless, they did have enough education to point out the flaws in the information they received and to ask questions they knew could not be answered. In fact, the Ministry of Interior had professional bureaucrats whose main job seems to have been to twist and distort the information in such a way as to ridicule the information source and to cow and silence those who transmitted such unpleasant information as that about famine. Reading through these letters, one cannot but feel convinced that high officials were annoyed and offended by information on famine in much the same manner as one reacts when abruptly awakened from a deep and blissful sleep.

The higher and lower administrative officials represented two entirely different worlds. The lower administrative officials, especially a *awraja* and *wereda* levels, were mostly traditional people who did not even pretend to have any idea of public service, but who, on the contrary, believed that they were only getting a reward for the services they rendered either to the country or to some high official, or who believed that the position they held was their birthright. Those in a higher position of authority, on the other hand, were people who knew better, and who had the notion that they were public servants who knew what was good for the people and for the country; in practice, however, they knew better for themselves. The only common characteristic between the two groups of officials was that they both used their public offices to promote their self-interest. In terms of their practical work, the basic difference between the two groups was that those at the lower level dealt directly with real people and their real problems, while those at the higher level of authority dealt only with paper.

The result was that information coming from the semi-literate and traditional lower-level administrators became too fragmentary, general, unintelligible and unconvincing to those above. Likewise, the questions and instructions that came from the modern and apparently educated higher authorities became incomprehensible and impractical to the lower officials. Unintelligible to each other, endless correspondence became their weapon for absolving themselves of any responsibility.

The flow of information was interrupted at practically every level. for clarification, for confirmation, or with some trivial question. Then gradually a point of time was reached when the whole issue of the content of the information was replaced by procedural questions. As bureaucracy took its time, the process of famine intensified and widened, resulting in more suffering and death.

Only one example suffices to demonstrate the problem of information flow and bureaucratic lethargy. In 1965 there was famine in several *awrajas* of Wello. The initial source of information for this famine was the Werre Ilu *Awraja* police.[12] About thirty days later, the information on famine had already reached the Ministry of Interior *via* the Department of Security, for it wrote asking for a clarification from Wello.[13] Then nothing happened for 215 days. For some unknown reason, the Ministry of Interior requested Wello once more for clarification of the information on famine on the 216th day.[14] Six days later, Wello informed the Ministry of Interior that, because of starvation, peasants were leaving their villages *en masse*.[15] Forty-six days later, this information from Wello was followed by a request for 47,636 quintals of grain to help the victims of famine.[16] Fourteen days later Wello notified the ministry of Interior that 2738 persons had died of famine in one *mikittil wereda* alone in Ambassel *Awraja*.[17] Twenty days later, or 332 days after the Werre Ilu police transmitted the initial information on famine, the information reached the Emperor through an irregular channel.[18] As was to be expected, by this time reports of famine deaths were coming from various parts of Wello. Perhaps it was with the intention of stopping these reports that the Ministry of Interior instructed Wello to send a list of the names of the people that died of famine.[19]

With respect to transmitting information on famine, the commendable service of the Ethiopian police force deserves mention. In spite of the fact that famine information went through the necessary routine, following the usual hierarchy—from *wereda* to *awraja* to *kifle hagher* to the Addis Ababa Police Headquarters to Public Security and, finally, to the Ministry of Interior—the police were very often the first to notify the Ministry of Interior. Invariably the Ministry of Interior, quoting the information from the police, requested for a clarification from the *kifle hagher*, which sent it to the *awraja* which passed it on to the *weredas*.

It is important to realize that if there had been goodwill on the part of higher officials, when they received information that was admittedly poor in quantity, they could immediately have sent their own investigators to the famine-affected areas and acquired the necessary information. But this assumes a sense of urgency which they completely lacked.

Decision and Action

In a highly centralized administrative set-up where the Emperor, at the top of the hierarchy, was the be-all and end-all, decision and action for individual officials could become a very painful problem. Servility and loyalty to him meant service, and his favour could bestow administrative competence on anyone.

In such conditions, officials of the government were preoccupied more with competition for the favour of the Emperor rather than with carrying on their administrative functions.

If, as we have already seen, it was difficult for government officials to transmit information that might displease the Emperor, to decide and to act on that information must have been much more difficult. In the first place, none of the officials in any of the administrative subdivisions of the country nor the Ministry of Interior itself had adequate financial resources at their disposal. Even if they had the financial resources, they could not use them without the authority of the Emperor. Consequently, in a famine situation, nobody but the Emperor could decide on any course of action.

The decision-making process related to transmitting famine information to the Emperor was long and laborious. All higher officials of the government were intimidated by it, since the Emperor did not have the reputation of receiving unpleasant information gracefully. But when events made the withholding of famine information from the Emperor more dangerous to them, the ministers would reach a decision to inform him. Even at this stage there was often a problem of whether the Minister of Interior or the Prime Minister should present a famine issue first to the Council of Ministers and, later, to the Emperor.[20] Once all these obstacles created by fear were overcome and the information reached the Emperor, some decision for action would be made.

But the authorized decision could rarely match the problem. In their desire not to displease the Emperor, the Ministers often presented the problem of famine with extreme caution and understatement. For instance, in the 1966 famine in Wello, when the information reached the Emperor as described above, the decision was to send 3,000 quintals of grain to be distributed free in all the famine-affected *awrajas* and an additional 6,000 quintals to be sold at 18 Birr per quintal.[21] It was only in exceptional circumstances that the Emperor, on the recommendation of the Council of

Ministers, ordered the delivery of more than 2,000 quintals of grain to a famine-stricken *awraja*.[22] If there were, say, 20,000 needy persons in a famine-stricken *awraja*, 2,000 quintals (which is 200,000 kgs.) could not last for more than about ten days; if there were 200,000 persons, it is hardly enough for three days. Meanwhile the suffering of the poor continued, some dying and some might be on the brink of death.

The decision of the Emperor was transmitted through the Ministry of Pen to the Ministry of Finance to make a given sum of money available, and to the Ministry of Agriculture to provide the grain. If, in the process of implementing the decision, some practical difficulties arose, the necessity of informing the Emperor for a further decision presented itself as a new formidable problem. After the initial decision was made, very often problems connected with transportation and insufficiency of the amount of grain became immediate issues. As a result, several months often elapsed before even the inadequate decision was translated into action.

A combination of several factors militated against swift decision and resolute action. First and foremost, there was the Emperor's reluctance and displeasure to hear any news about famine in his fertile kingdom. The second important factor was bureaucratic timidity and indifference, sheer incompetence and irresponsibility, as well as a possessive fear of losing favour with the Emperor. The third and actually important factor was the attitude of the rural people, the victims of famine, both towards famine and towards political authority. Their understanding of famine as an act of God exonerated the political system and the ruling class, and turned their attention away from the realm of the possible. This attitude became the source of an almost inexhaustible patience in the face of extreme hardship and suffering.

All these factors were but the distinct and definite manifestations of the structural deformity of the political system. The Emperor, believed to derive his authority from God, felt no legal or constitutional responsibility or accountability to the people. Being above the law, he was the fountain of law and authority. He appointed not only the higher officials of government, but also governor-generals, *awraja* adminstrators, and sometimes even *wereda* administrators. All officials, therefore, considered themselves accountable only to him. The Prime Minister had a responsibility for, but not the authority

over the Cabinet. Similarly, the Minister of Interior was responsible for provincial administration, but almost any authority
over the officials presumed to be under him. That officials at various
levels of government administration derived their authority from
the same ultimate source created a bottleneck that rendered the
machinery of state subject to attrition by endless friction, for it
lacked any lubricating mechanism. The ignominious manner of its
swift collapse in the face of social forces that rose against it testifies,
against all shades of opinion, to its lack of any foundation. It provided one more historical lesson for human societies, namely, that
no one man, whatever the claim for the source of his authority, can
misrule a nation to death by famine and get away with it. We must,
however, return to our immediate task of demonstrating the role of
government in precipitating a condition of famine.

In the case we cited, the 1966 famine in Wello, the first information on famine was, as already stated, transmitted by the Werre
Ilu police about the middle of October 1965. It is reasonable to
assume, given a responsive and responsible administrative system,
that crop failure, due to whatever natural cause, could have been
foreseen at least 90 days earlier. But even after the report of the
Werre Ilu police, it took 332 days for the information to reach the
Emperor, and Wello was a region which had the Crown Prince, the
Emperor's son, as its ruler. The Emperor's decision was as disastrous as the delay in the information flow. When the officials in
Wello had requested 47,636 quintals of grain for only five, *awrajas*
the Emperor authorized only 3000 quintals in the relief aid and 6000
quintals in subsidized partial aid for twelve *awrajas*. It took months
to translate even this unhelpful decision into action. Since the
decision was tantamount to allowing the process of famine to go
through its full course, even if action followed decision more
swiftly, in this case it would have been impossible to arrest the
consequent death by famine of thousands of persons.

Resources, Society and Poverty

Resources are created by people in order to meet their basic and
immediate needs, as well as those needs that are subsequently
created by them. Nature provides the raw materials from which
resources are created. From this point of view, therefore, man is
not only the consumer of resources but also their creator. Opportunities and limitations for creating resources are found in both

the natural and the socio-economic conditions.

The elements of physical nature vary from place to place. These variations in the elements of physical nature partly account for differences in opportunities and limitations for the creation of resources.[23] Where the conditions of physical nature are so harsh and poor that they hardly provide man with opportunities to satisfy even his basic needs, the limitations become more pronounced. But where conditions are such that man can more or less easily satisfy his basic needs, the opportunities stand out more prominently than the limitations. In other words, opportunities and limitations exist for all societies; but the degree to which one overshadows the other will, at least partly, depend on the conditions of the physical environment.

But this at once raises questions over the fact, that some richly endowed areas are inhabited by very poor people and some poorly endowed areas by relatively rich people. We have said that man is not only the consumer of resources but also, more importantly, their creator. It is that function of creation, or the lack of it, which becomes, in the social realm, the measure of opportunities and limitations. The opportunities provided and the limitations imposed by society are, therefore, more crucial than those of physical nature. If the function of creation is arrested in a society, then that society has no way of perceiving the opportunities provided by physical nature. It can only grope in the darkness of limitations, with no vision of a nature that can be different.

John Stuart Mill, in his essay on *Liberty*, states the following important point:

> ...a State which dwarfs its men, in order that they may be more docile instruments in its hands even for beneficial purposes, will find that with small men no great thing can really be accomplished; and that the perfection of the machinery to which it has sacrificed everything will in the end avail it nothing, for want of the vital power which, in order that the machine might work more smoothly, it has preferred to banish.[24]

What we refer to as limitations are that "want of the vital power". It is not, however, only the state machinery that stifles the vital power. Sociocultural, including religious, values play a part in incapacitating man's vital power. Conformity to fossilized values and norms as well as fear of the consequences of dissent considerably reduce the opportunity for enlarging the society's capacity for change. The society's capacity for change grows with freedom—with freedom from oppession, exploitation and want, as well as with freedom for the dialectical development of its intellectual and material resources creatively.

A government that severely restricts the mental and creative potential of its citizens on any ground condemns the whole society and its own self to backwardness and poverty, for, in the final analysis, unwittingly, that society has declared as its motto: "It is forbidden to think." This is the ultimate limitation that a government can impose upon the society and upon itself. That is partly why advisers, that is to say, men with special privileges and licence to think, abound in the so-called underdeveloped countries.

As Engles has emphasized, while "the conservative side" of dialectics "recognizes that definite stages of knowledge and society are justified for their time and circumstances", its "revolutionary character", which is "the only absolute dialectical philosophy admits",[25] does nothing but reveal "the transitory character of everything and in everything",[26] destroying the foundation of any absolute truth and, in its place, constructing the basis for a scientific attitude.

Even if physical nature is bountiful, an adverse socio-economic and political condition constricts a society into moral and material decay and poverty. In such a society, three contributary factors of stagnation may be singled out. The concentration of power in the hands of a small minority, which may be traditional or modern, generates two processes that will in the long run keep the society stagnant. One is the proliferation of new needs on the part of the ruling minority, and the other is the ever-increasing burden on the masses of the people to pay for the excessive comfort of the ruling elite. Marx expresses this idea by saying, "The multiplication of needs and of the means of their satisfaction breeds the absence of needs and of means . . ." by "reducing the worker's need to the barest and most miserable level of physical subsistence."[27] In the words of Lewis Mumford, which are even more pertinent to this context than the one in which he wrote them, "Misery at the bottom becomes the foundation for luxury at the top."[28] The wretched conditions of living and the severe and exigent demands of the basic needs reduce the majority of the people to servile rivalry for the favour and charity of the minority which, on its parts, engrossed in the competition for the satisfaction of its own proliferating needs, grows insensitive to the misery of the majority. The two processes converge to the same end: poverty dehumanizing the masses and the insensitivity of power dehumanizing the minority. R.H. Tawney expresses this idea as follows:

> . . . poverty is a symptom and a consequence of social disorder, while the disorder itself is something at once more fundamental and more incorrigible, and that quality in their social life which causes it to demoralize a few by excessive riches is also the quality which causes it to demoralize many by excessive poverty.[29]

Social disorder is the first factor of stagnation manifesting itself in a general condition that is oppressive, unresponsive, and backward.

The two other factors are corollaries of the first. One factor is the merciless exploitation of the masses, of which the peasants form the vast majority. "The main function of the state [in underdeveloped countries]", says Duverger, "is to maintain the domination of a privileged minority which exploits the masses."[30] In fact, Duverger states that underdeveloped countries are "condemned to authoritarian regimes",[31] which means to permanent exploitation and poverty. If imitation of the consumption habits of the developed countries is taken as a sign of modernization, as long as the ruling elite modernize (which is nothing more than developing the taste and the appetite for the latest consumption goods, at a rate that the productive capacity of the masses cannot cope with), then abject poverty will certainly remain a characteristic feature of the countries in the Third World.

The third factor is reliance on foreign aid. This reliance is pervasive, so pervasive that it does not even spare the intellectual and spiritual life of a society. Foreign aid is required to think, to identify the problems of the society and to formulate solutions for them, to work out projects, to determine priorities, and to finance them. Very often it is not the real and crying needs of the masses of people that determine projects involving foreign aid, but what the donor countries can and are willing to dispose of. This is at least one of the major reasons for the ineffectiveness of foreign aid.

It is important to bear in mind that foreign aid, as such, is not inconsequential. What makes it inconsequential, or even harmful, is the inability of the recipients to determine their own needs and priorities, and to insist on aid for specific purposes, on one hand, and the desire of the donors to create new needs and to strengthen the dependence of the recipients on them, on the other. It is the fact that most foreign aid is determined not by the needs of the recipient countries but by the needs of the donor countries that makes it ineffective. Foreign aid does not scratch where the itch is. In the words of an Ethiopian poet:

When I feel the itch on my head, to scratch my foot
Serves me no purpose and helps me not one bit.[32]

The foregoing discussion leads us to conclude that poverty and stagnation are primarily limitations that emanate from social disorder, the occasional adverse condition of physical nature serving only to emphasize the limitations of socio-economic and political institutions. While we cannot ignore the role of government in the general poverty of a given population in a given country its particular role in famine, which is but one of the extreme manifestations of general poverty, is what concerns us more.

In what we have been discussing so far, the role of the government in famine took two forms, acts of commission and acts of omission. The impoverishment and degradation of rural life was due to continuous exploitation in various ways by officials of the government and landlords. Officials were carefully selected not for what they could do for the people, but for what they could squeeze out of the peasants to fill the government treasury as well as their own. The rural people were there to be milked mercilessly. The collusion between government functionaries and traditional leaders became an insufferable burden to the rural masses of Ethiopia. The government's arsenal of war could be used brutally against those who lost the great Ethiopian virtue of patience, as the peasants in Gojjam, Yejju, and Ghidewo (Derasa), amongst many, vividly remember.

This is not a post-mortem, or a futile exercise to beat a dead horse. The following statement, expressed in 1968, may have fallen on deaf ears:

The Ethiopian peasants have no organization of any kind and therefore have no voice. The only way they could traditionally express their grievances was by either standing at the gate of the Palace and crying out in unison, *abet!* or by intercepting the Emperor on the road. For obvious reasons this is becoming less and less possible and the frustrations of the peasants may find other outlets. To the rural populations, the government comes to them only to collect taxes and does not bring them anything in return. They feel neglected, alienated and robbed.[33]

It was stated even more bluntly at a public meeting at Africa Hall exactly one year before the downfall of the *ancien regime*:

If we say there is government (defined as an organization that is committed to improving the well-being of the people) in Ethiopia we will be deceiving only ourselves. It will be nearer the truth to say that we have an executive committee of a share company with unlimited irresponsibility.[34]

The "insatiable greed and blind exploitation"[35] that is rampant found the rural masses a silent and easy prey.

The rural masses were painfully aware of their misery and of the greed of their exploiters. Gaetano Salvemini observed in relation to the French peasants, "It was the Government rather than the weather, to which they owed their misery."[36] Ethiopian peasants rarely articulated their grievances. One peasant in northern Shewa, after being prodded for about two hours on his condition of living, stopped his ploughing oxen and said with a calm indignation:

You think we are lazy, perhaps. We are not. You see how we toil, and we are prepared to toil more. But the more we get the greater becomes the appetite of those who live on us. You know, we are like this earth (he said stamping his foot), we are silent fools. This earth—you can plough it, can dig it, you can spit on it, you can throw any waste or refuse on it, you can do anything. It does not complain. We are the same.[37]

That this peasant perceived a very close affinity between Ethiopian peasants and the "silent earth", the only source of their sustenance, is revealing, perhaps, more for the manner and the articulation than for the substance that is widely understood. A more important point, however, is his allusion to "the more we get the greater becomes the appetite of those who live on us",[38] which led him to the conclusion that since he was not master of his own produce, it was fruitless to toil for more. It was not only the earth and the peasants that were silent, we may join Carlyle in saying: "Earth's Laws are silent; and Heaven's speak in a voice which is not heard."[39]

Basically the government's role in famine, in form of commission, lay in its accentuating the vulnerability of the peasants through direct and indirect oppression and exploitation. The peasants clearly recognized this problem, if we are allowed to generalize from information on only a few *weredas*. About 50% of the peasants felt that "the most serious problem in dealing with Government officials" was "corruption and bribery".[40] Even more telling is the fact that about 20% of them felt that "What the central government should do for local inhabitants" was improve administration, law and order (police) legal services (courts), control corruption, and provide defence.[41] That means that one out of every five peasants felt that the government would do the greatest service to the people by improving itself, rather than by attempting to tackle the problems of agricultural development, pest control, infrastructure and factory construction, and marketing agricultural products, all of these indicated as possible answers. One-fifth of the peasants were in fact telling the government that they knew how to manage their business if only the government knew how to manage its own. It is also interesting to observe that in the *weredas* of famine-prone regions, the proportion of peasants with that view rose to as high as 36%.

The government's role in famine, by its acts of omission, was equally important. Famine is a catastrophic process, not a catastrophic event. The long process of famine which started with a worsening food shortage in a rural condition unavailable reserves of grain or cash was allowed to continue, often for a year or longer, to reach its full maturity of mass annihilation. All this time, government bureaucracy would be exchanging irrelevant letters without any sense of urgency. In Chapter Second we have attempted to demonstrate this bureaucratic indifference, treating famine only as a matter of routine. The failure of higher authorities of government to make the appropriate decisions in time, and their failure to organize public support for effective relief effort are what constitute the government's sin of omission.

Vulnerability to famine is a combined effect of the government's acts of commission and of omission. It is on this vulnerability to famine that natural factors act.

NOTES

[1]John Locke. ed. Peter Laslett, *Two Treatises of Government,* (A Mentor Book, New York, 1965), pp. 376-377.

[2]Jean Jacques Rousseau, trans. and G.D.H. Cole, *The Social Contract Discourses,* (Everyman's Library, London, 1958), p. 13.

[3]Thomas Hobbes, ed. C.B. Macpherson, *Laviathan,* (Penguin, Aylesbury, 1968), pp. 228-238.

[4]See R.M. MacIver, *The Modern State,* (London, 1964), and T.D. Weldon, *States and Morals: A Study in Political Conflicts,* (London, 1962).

[5]John Locke, *op. cit.,* p. 448.

[6]Jean Jacques Rousseau, *op. cit.,* p. 65.

[7]London 1941, p. i.

[8]*Ibid.,* p. v.

[9]The literal translation is: What God said the people said, and what the people said God said.

[10]Marx and Engels, *Selected Works,* (Moscow, 1973), Vol. I. p. 35. Elaborate exposition of this view is found in V.I. Lenin, *The State and Revolution,* (Peking 1965).

[11]The largest administrative unit the Administrative Region, was called *Teqlay Ghizat* before the Revolution. Now it is *kifle hagher.*

[12]Werre Ilu *Awaraja* Police to Wello Police, 2/4/57.

[13]Ministry of Interior, quoting the Department of Security, to Wello, 24/3/57.

[14]Ministry of Interior to Wello, 30/10/57.

[15]Wello to Ministry of Interior, 6/11/57.

[16]Wello to Ministry of Interior, 22/12/57.

[17]Wello to Ministry of Interior, 22/1/58.

[18]The Emperor was informed on 26/1/58, and the letter from Ministry of Pen to Ministry of Finance was sent on 27/1/58.

[19]Ministry of Interior to Wello, 4/2/58.

[20]Prime Minister's Office to Ministry of Interior, 13/2/61.

[21]Ministry of Pen to Ministry of Finance, 27/1/58.

[22]Commission of Inquiry, *op. cit.,* p. 9.

[23]A slightly different view based on stress and opportunity is expounded by Len Berry, "Dynamics and Processes of Rural Change," eds. C. Gregory Knight and James L. Newman, *Contemporary Africa: Geography and Change,* (Englewood Cliffs, 1976).

[24]John Stuart Mill, *Utilitarianism, Liberty and Representative Government,* (London, 1948), p. 170.

[25]Karl Marx and Frederick Engels, *Selected Works*, Vol. 3, p. 340.

[26]*Ibid.*, p. 330. See also p. 131.

[27]Karl Marx, *Economic and Philosophic Manuscripts of 1844*, ed. Dirk S. Srink, trans. Martin Milligan, (New York, 1973), p. 149.

[28]Lewis Mumford, *The City in History*, (New York, 1961), p. 432.

[29]R.H. Tawney, *op. cit.*, p. 5.

[30]Maurice Duverger, trans. Robert North and Ruth Murphy, *The Idea of Politics: The Uses of Power in a Society*, (a University Paperback, London, 1964), p. 199.

[31]*Ibid.*, p. 218.

[32]My own translation from Kebbede Mikael, *Tarikinna Missale*, (in Amharic).

[33]Mesfin Wolde-Mariam, "Rural-Urban Split in Ethiopia" *Dialogue*, A Publication of Ethiopian University Teachers' Association, (Addis Ababa, December 1968), Vol. II, No. 1, p. 13.

[34]Mesfin Wolde-Mariam, "The Task of Government in Rural Development" (a talk delivered at the Seminar on Rural Ethiopia, organized by the Alumni Association, from 22-24 February 1973, in Amharic), my own translation. Obviously it could not be published.

[35]Mesfin Wolde-Mariam, Rural-Urban Split, *op. cit.*, p. 12.

[36]Gaetano Salvemini, *The French Revolution: 1788-1792*, (London, 1965), p. 120.

[37]Mesfin Wolde-Mariam, "Cultural Problems of Development", a paper presented to the Seminar of Ethiopian Studies, Faculty of Arts, HSIU (Addis Ababa, 1966), pp. 6-7. There is an interesting similarity between the words of this peasant and those of the Italian peasant who told Edward C. Banfield: "We poor peasants...work from morning until night, always touching the earth and always covered with mud", *op. cit.*, p. 65.

[38]In fact, the word he used was "hyena".

[39]Thomas Carlyle, *Past and Present*, (Everyman's Library, London, 1947), p. 211.

[40]Fassil G. Kiros and Assefa Mehretu, *op. cit.*, my own calculation from the data presented.

[41]*Loc cit.*

PART IV

EXPLANATIONS OF FAMINE

Chapter Six

Conventional Explanations of Famine

Famine has been the misfortune of mankind since time immemorial. There are, perhaps, only a very few countries that may have escaped the horrors of famine. People have therefore always attempted to understand and to explain this persistent and pernicious phenomenon of famine. We shall now review the major explanations of famine.

Drought

Very often famine is simply explained away by drought. But what is drought? It may first be instructive to have an idea of aridity, a sort of permanent drought. As yet there is no universally acceptable and applicable definition of aridity. Walten, before reviewing the various indices of aridity states:

Since aridity is primarily a function of rainfall, temperature and evaporation, it is wrong to define it in terms of one parameter alone, although average annual rainfall totals have been frequently used as a simple index of aridity. Some workers have taken the margin of the inner arid zone as the 127 mm (5 in) isohyet. The southern margin of the Sahara was drawn where the annual rainfall is 250 mm (9, 8 in) and the equatorial margin of the semi-arid savana at the 400 mm (15.7 in) isohyet. These are, however, oversimplifications which ignore the influence of temperature on the efficiency of precipitation but may be of value if the isohyet chosen is related to a change in the character of the vegetation, land-use or way of life. In this respect the 400 mm (15.7 in) isohyet, said to define the southern limit of the North African Arid Zone, is of significance. To the north of this isohyet agriculture cannot take place without irrigation, the need for which is frequently used to define the arid lands.[1]

Then he concludes on a rather unhappy note:

Enough has been said to indicate the problems and difficulties of delimiting the arid and semi-arid areas. The fact remains that for at least one-third of the land area of the globe lack of moisture is the limiting factor for vegetation, animal life and land-use. Plants, animals and human beings must adapt themselves to an existence where they are constantly faced with the problem of water shortage, often under extremely high temperature regimes. In so doing, a complex physical/biological relationship is established, a dynamic relationship which betrays a constant adjustment to changes in precipitation and evaporation and makes the arid environment of vital interest.[2]

More or less the same view is expressed by Gilbert White:

There are no clear boundaries of the arid lands. There are as many lines on maps as there are measures of aridity in climate, plants, land forms and soils. Yet, the arid lands may be thought of as having in common a sparsity of rainfall and a high variability of rainfall. Sparsity and variability are the characteristics of the arid zone which show themselves everywhere in uneven patterns of streams, vegetation, and people.[3]

Why is it difficult to define aridity in terms of the natural condition of rainfall, temperature, and soil? It is, perhaps, because aridity is a human conception that is inseparably tied to the mode of making a living and to the cultural level of societies. When we speak of aridity we do not often think of the natural conditions objectively, but in terms of their effect on man. It is, therefore, the variations in the actions of man at different cultural levels and the consequent variations in the effects of the natural conditions that defy definition.[4]

Similarly, there is not yet, it seems, a generally accepted definition of drought. What percentage below the average annual rainfall will constitute drought? Is it possible that, the annual amount of rainfall remaining more or less normal, the rainfall season may shift backward or forward to produce drought? Is it possible for the rains to occur in such heavy showers in an unusually shorter duration that loss by run-off becomes greater, resulting in reduced soil moisture irrespective of total amount of rainfall? So how do we define drought? Wisner, quoting Kaltenhauser, defines drought as "a meteorological excursion from normal of sufficient size and duration as to cause serious damage to the established plant, animal, or human life system."[5] He also quotes another definition of drought which is presumed to be similar to the one quoted. This second definition states that "a period of water shortage becomes a drought only when cultural or biologic activity becomes constricted."[6]

Let us first take Kaltenhauser's definition of drought. The definition begs the question. To state that drought is a "meteorological excursion from normal of sufficient size and duration" is to tell us nothing, for it is precisely "the size and duration" that we want to know. The problem of attempting to define drought in general ignores important local or even regional variations and consequently fails to be helpful to specific cases. A definition of drought may be helpful if it includes statements on people, and to the critical amount of rainfall during the growing period of different plants. Kaltenhauser's definition of drought leaves out all these crucial characteristics by employing too general a phrase, "sufficient size and duration".

The second part of Kaltenhauser's definition renders it even more subjective. Not only is it left to the reader to determine "the size and duration" of the unusual meteorological condition, it is also left to him to determine the nature and magnitude of the "serious damage" to plant, animal, and human "life systems". How much drought will bring how much damage will depend not only on the natural conditions but also on the socio-economic and political organization of societies. We all knew that droughts have occurred in the United States and some parts of Europe. We also know that no serious damage has followed drought in these countries. A similar drought elsewhere in the world may have had catastrophic consequences. Objectively speaking, the drought that occurs in the United States or Western Europe may not in any way be different from the drought that takes place in Africa and in Asia. "Serious damage" to plant, animal and human "life systems" does take place now after drought in Africa and in Asia, but does not take place in the United States or Western Europe. This fact seems to suggest that drought as a purely natural condition must be separated from the possible consequences of drought into which human action or inaction enters. That this is so is illustrated by the following statements of Sandford:

> Britain, in 1976, experienced rainfall which was variously described as being the lowest for 200, 500, or even 1000 years. The consequent 'drought' led to the closure or restriction to part-time working of a number of industrial concerns, as a result of failure or shortages of urban water supplies. The urban population of Britain was universally aware of the drought, which it regarded as quite exceptional. Britain's agriculture, in contrast, was relatively little affected. Cereal yields in 1976 were higher than in the 1950's and less than twenty per cent down on what could have been expected if the rainfall in 1976 had been normal. The yields of the main vegetable crops, other than potatoes, were scarcely affected at all. I suggest that to many British farmers 1976 was not really a drought year at all.[7]

It is quite understandable that it is extremely difficult to define drought because the characteristics of the rainfall, soil, types, land form, and plant types vary from place to place. Even in the same country local variations can be so significant that it will be very difficult, if not impossible, to define drought for the country as a whole. For instance, in the southwestern parts of Ethiopia where the rainfall is heavy and is distributed through most of the year, a reduction of, let us say, 20% of the average annual rainfall may not significantly affect plant growth. On the other hand, a reduction of 5% or less from the total amount of average annual rainfall in the drier parts of eastern and southeastern Ethiopia may have, it seems, disastrous consequences. This is partly the reason why it is difficult to have a comprehensive and objective definition of drought.

W.C. Palmer lists some seven definitions of drought and comments that the list "could be extended, but nearly all have in common a certain arbitrariness difficult, in some cases, to defend."[8] His own definition is:

> A drought period may now be defined as an interval of time, generally of the order of months or years in duration, during which the actual moisture supply at a given place rather consistently falls short of the climatically expected or climatically appropriate moisture supply. Further, the severity of drought may be considered as being a function of both the duration and magnitude of the moisture deficiency.[9]

This definition, too, fails to state any critical limit, if any, below which drought may be considered severe. It is doubtful, too, whether "moisture deficiency" is the result of drought alone.[10]

Sandford has suggested a completely different definition, namely, that drought is "a rainfall-induced shortage of some economic good, . . . brought about by inadequate or badly timed rainfall."[11] The phrase "rainfall-induced shortage" accentuates dependence and a lack of an alternative leading to an assumption of a relatively low level of development, while "economic good" seems to refer almost exclusively to a market economy. Moreover, the definition suggests that food shortage is causally related to inadequate or badly timed rainfall, a very questionable notion.

We must, therefore, recognize the problem of defining drought. A universally applicable definition of drought is not yet in sight. There is little doubt, however, that such a definition must take into account the complexity of the socio-economic and political organization of societies and the consequent variations in the effects of climatological changes.

That is why it becomes necessary to be very careful not to confuse drought with famine. It has already been indicated that in the developed countries of the world drought is never associated with famine. There have been several cases of drought in southwestern United States, but none of them were followed by famine. Britain, France, and China have had famines in the more or less recent past. These countries are free from the menace of famine today. This does not suggest a change in the meteorological condition. Moreover, there are poor and economically backward countries for which drought is not a temporary but a permanent condition. Here, too, famine is not a permanent feature, mainly because the condition of permanent drought is accepted as normal and the people, as well as their animals, anticipating nothing more than the normal, adjust themselves to it, mainly by leading a frugal and delicately balanced existence. In dry nomadic areas the process of famine may be initiated not only by a reduction of the grass cover due to drought. We must bear in mind that the reduction of the grass cover may occur as a result of overgrazing as well. It appears, therefore, that drought alone does not explain famine even if we were able to define it and ascertain its presence. It is only under certain conditions that drought can become one of the factors of famine.

It will certainly be reasonable to state that wherever cultivation is totally dependent on rainfall, not only a significant reduction of the rainfall but also its occurrence at the wrong time may bring about crop failure. Drought may or may not be the cause of crop failure. It may also result from human failure to anticipate drought and provide an alternative. Whatever the reason for crop failure, we can only infer an impending food shortage which may or may not lead to famine, depending on the political, social, and economic condition of the people affected. Quite obviously where, for one reason or another, crop failure leads to food shortage which is not alleviated by local food reserves or by supplies from other areas, famine will take its natural course. The question that we must ask, therefore, is why do some societies fail to anticipate drought and make the necessary arrangements? Is famine, then, a consequence of drought or of the society's failure to adjust to a recurring natural phenomenon? Since permanent drought in some countries and occasional drought in others does not necessarily result in famine, the association between drought and famine in only some countries is, indeed, questionable. It is hard to believe that peasants and nomads, if they were left alone, will fail to adjust themselves to, or to devise some mechanism against, the danger of crop failure.

In Ethiopia there is a remarkable and obvious fact in the distribution of the population in relation to rainfall. The lower, hotter, and drier parts of the country are occupied by nomadic pastoralists, whereas the higher, wetter, and relatively cool areas are occupied by farming people. The correlation between nomadic pastoralists and rainfall is —0.61, whereas the correlation between farming people and rainfall is +0.39. This fact seems to indicate the greater dependence of farming on rainfall.

The available rainfall data are neither sufficient in quantity nor satisfactory in quality. Because of variations of altitude, in position in relation to the direction of the moisture-bearing winds, in temperature, and of evaporation both the total amount of rainfall and effective rainfall show marked differences within short distances. These variations make it very difficult to determine the typical meteorological station for a whole *awraja*.

Using the available data, however, we encounter some serious difficulties in consistently relating famine to drought. For instance, in the two years preceding the two consecutive regional famine in Tigray, in 1958 and in 1959, the mean annual rainfall in Meqele in 1957 was 102% of the average, and there are no data for 1958. Similarly, for the regional famine of 1966 in Tigray, the annual rainfall for 1965 was only 6% lower than the average. When there were five *awrajas* under famine in Tigray in 1965, the rainfall in the previous year was 129%. Similarly, the regional famine of 1973 in Tigray was preceded by a year with a rainfall of 101%. Obviously, the total amount of rainfall was adequate if we take the average as a measurement. (See *Figure 5.*)

The total rainfall in Asmera in 1958 was 100.2% of the average, and yet, in the following year, 1959, there was regional famine in Eritrea. Similarly, in 1964 the total rainfall for Asmera was 112.3% of the average, and again there was regional famine in Eritrea in 1965. It is true that the rainfall in Asmera is not an indicator of the rainfall in Eritrea as a whole. If we take Aqordat, in the western drier lowland of Eritrea, the total rainfall in 1958 was 6% below the average, and in 1966 it was lower by about 11%. This might suggest that the famine in Aqordat *Awraja* might have been related rainfall. But the relationship between famine and rainfall in Hamasen *Awraja* is at least doubtful.

If we take Wello as another example, our possible inference will improve only slightly. The total rainfall in Kembolcha in 1964 was 128% of the average, and there was regional famine in 1965. But the 1973 famine in Wello seems to be preceded by drought, because total rainfall in 1971 and in 1972 was 84.6 and 84.0% of the average, respectively.

It is, therefore, very difficult to conclude that drought is the cause of famine. Even if it is established that drought invariably precedes famine, we cannot from this conclude that drought and famine are causally related. What begs for explanation is the period between

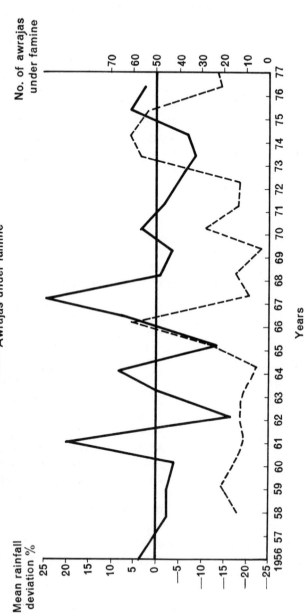

DROUGHT AND FAMINE

MEAN RAINFALL DEVIATION %, 1956—1977
AND FAMINE, 1958—1977

—— Mean rainfall deviation
----- Awrajas under famine

Mean rainfall
deviation %

No. of awrajas
under famine

Years

FIGURE 5

the time when drought is recognized and the commencement of the period of starvation. It is this period of waiting passively that *allows* the process of famine to develop to its full capacity of destruction. There should be no doubt that in some countries, drought leads to crop failure. What is challenged, here, is the prevalent notion that crop failure almost automatically leads to famine.

It is not to be forgotten, however, that drought is not the only natural factor that may bring about crop failure. Plant and animal diseases, pests, frost, and numerous other natural processes may be important factors of crop failure. The presence or absence of any mechanism for controlling these natural factors is in the realm of social responsibility. If and when in the absence of any mechanism of control, crop failure occurs, then again the absence of any alternative arrangement of food supply and the long process that leads to famine is in the sphere of social responsibility.

Political Explanations

The political explanations of famine are best exemplified by the two books *How the Other Half Dies* by Susan George, and *Food First* by Frances Moore Lappe and Joseph Collins. For two reasons it may be said that these two books, written generally with reason and passion, have rendered a very valuable service: first, these books contain valuable information on the subject of food shortage, hunger, and famine covering most of the world both in time and space; second, they have forcefully shattered some of the established myths on famine. There is no doubt, therefore, that Susan George, Frances Moore Lappe and Joseph Collins have made valuable contributions.

The wealth of information the three authors have gathered, the articulation, and the passionate reason follow in the footsteps of De Castro and Dumont. They are also similar in their undifferentiated treatment of hunger, malnutrition and undernourishment, on one hand, and famine, on the other. Since we have already dealt with this problem earlier we shall not return to it.

The two books cited have however, unfortunately aslo started another myth. For them colonialism and neo-colonialism are responsible at least for the present outbreak of famine in various parts of the world. For these writers and several others, the *bete blance* of colonialism serves to explain away the pernicious and apparently eternal problem of famine. One line of argument is that colonialism "stunted indigenous agriculture by directing agricultural research only to export crops.'[12] The other line of argument is the abundance of wealth and overconsumption in the industrialized countries which are held to be "responsible"[13] for the famine in the Third World, either because they feed their animals with precious grain that would have saved human lives in the poor countries, or because they promote the production of cash crops which they buy at very cheap prices. Apart from exploitation, colonialism reduced the land under food crops by sometimes persuading and sometimes forcing peasants to grow cash crops for which there was a demand in the metropolitan or world markets. It is important to bear in mind that the charges against colonialism are not limited to what it did, but also cover what it did not do, such as not directing agricultural research to food crops. One writer has indeed gone as far as to state that in Tanganyika "famine problems were far less prevalent in pre-colonial period than they became later".[14]

This may very well have been the case in Tanganyika, although it may be difficult to establish that peculiarity. The problem, here, however, is not whether or not there are exceptional cases, but whether or not the assertion that colonialism in general is the origin of famine can stand any closer scrutiny.

The alleged responsibility of the developed countries for the famine in the Third World is equally disturbing. The arguments jump freely from moral to political to economic and back to moral norms. The main thrust of the argument rests on what the developed countries do or do not do in relation to the underdeveloped countries. For instance, the question whether pigs are "more important than people"[15] implies a moral or some idealistic norm, whereas the statement that "food-deficit countries must reduce their dependency on the West"[16] sounds like down-to-earth realism. The moral judgement is lucidly expressed by Rene Dumont.

> The rich white man, with his overconsumption of meat and his lack of generosity for poor people behaves like a veritable cannibal —an indirect cannibal. By consuming meat, which wastes the grain that would have saved them, last year we ate the children of Sahel, Ethiopia and Bangladesh. And we continue to eat them this year with undiminished appetite.[17]

Needless to say this sort of excessively immoderate articulation of a peculiar moral judgement contributes nothing to our understanding of famine, nor does it help us in our search for solutions.

Such arguments directed at colonialism, or to the developed countries as a whole or to the West in particular, or to the white man, are as disturbing as they are unconvincing. They are disturbing because they emphatically misplace responsibility for famine on exogenous elements. They are unconvincing because the confusion in these arguments is matched only by the zeal and piquancy with which they are presented. Inadequate knowledge about the internal conditions of underdeveloped countries is compensated by the more readily accessible and abundant knowledge of the developed countries. As a result, the underdeveloped countries are treated *in terms* of the developed countries. For instance, Susan George's question, "Are pigs more important than people?" implies the very unpleasant fact that starving people in underdeveloped countries are worse off than pigs in the United States or the Soviet Union. The point, however, is that there occur also in the underdeveloped countries too, cats and dogs, pigs and cows, horses and mules that are better fed than the starving people, and there is hardly any need to concern oneself with American or Soviet pigs. And the question is, why do we expect the farms in the United States or the Soviet Union, as Susan George demands, to give up feeding their pigs with grain when in those very countries of famine the same thing, with only a change of scale, goes on?

Susan George could very well have asked: "Is beer more important than people?" Feeding grain to pigs is a mechanism of converting not only carbohydrates into animal protein but also of converting a relatively cheap commodity into a rather expensive one. For those who raise pigs, therefore, the question of whether or not pigs are more important than people is determined not by any moral principle but by the market. We must be careful not to confuse the ideal with the reality. To understand the reality is not to condone it. The reality was sharply stated by R.H. Tawney in his outstanding work, *The Acquisitive Society*:

. . . the perversion of nationalism is imperialism, as the perversion of individualism is industrialism. And the perversion comes, not through any flaw or vice in human nature, but by the force of the idea, because the principle is defective and reveals its defects as it reveals its power. For it asserts that the rights of

nations and individuals are absolute, which is false, instead of
asserting that they are absolute in their own sphere but that their
sphere itself is contigent upon the part which they play in the community of nations and individuals, which is true. Thus it constrains
them to a career of continents and oceans, law morality and
religion, and last of all their own souls, in an attempt to attain
infinity by the addition to themselves of all that is finite.[18]

There is one other observation that must be made in connection
with the arguments outlined above. Famine is explained in terms
of the actions and inactions of colonial powers of the developed
countries or the white man, so that the people of the Third World
are absolved of all responsibility for their chronic malaise. The
peoples and governments of the Third World are mere objects that
cannot be called upon to account for their own ills. They are only
there to be manipulated by this or that master mind. Such implicitly
condescending arguments are extremely dangerous, dangerous
because they incapacitate the peoples, especially the ruling elite of
the Third World, from accepting the responsibility for their own
condition, and for their own actions and inactions. In the face of
it, the arguments are intended to reduce the dependency of the
Third World. But the effect may be exactly the contrary, for it
appears that the first prerequisite for independence is the acceptance
of a large measure of responsibility for one's own condition. By
rationalizing one's mistakes, failures and inaptitude, and by passing
on the burden of responsibility to the bogeyman, it will be difficult,
if not altogether impossible, to get out of childish insecurity and
dependence.

That there was the most brutal form of exploitation under
colonialism is not to be disputed. The damage that colonialism has
done is not only material and economic, but perhaps even more
importantly, psychological. We can all agree on that. It is pertinent
to ask, however, how many years of colonialism does it take to
incapacitate a people for decades? How many years of independence
does it take to grow out of the devastating colonial heritage? In the
case of Ethiopia, it will be difficult, without twisting the historical
record, to blame the recurrent famine on the *bete blanche* of
colonialism. In the first place, the chronicles and other historical
documents going back over many centuries describe the horrors of
famine that occurred long before the advent of colonialism. Second,

it may be too much to make the five years of Italian half-rule accountable for the following thirty-five to forty years of Ethiopian misrule and the history of famine. Nor is it possible to blame it on the development of cash crops, which occupy a very insignificant proportion of the cultivated land. Nor is it possible to explain it in terms of export only.

A colonial administration pursues a policy of merciless exploitation, and this renders the society at large, the rural population in particular, vulnerable to famine. But at the same time and in order to make exploitation more rewarding, colonialism forces the people into a cash economy and commercializes farming. This is progressive. Whether or not the commercialization of agricultural production introduces advantages to rural populations will depend on the form and magnitude of exploitation. The introduction of cash crops enables farmers to produce high-value crops on the same plots which formerly were used for low-value food crops whenever natural conditions allow this change. This is progressive and certainly preferable, provided cash crop farmers derive real benefits from their new activity, and provided food crops are available at reasonable prices. But if the grains of cash crop farming are offset by increased exploitation and rising food prices, then they remain, in spite of commercialization, under subsistence system of production. This is a peculiarity of colonial administration, since it can happen under various non-colonial political systems. The crux of the matter, therefore, is that it is exploitation that creates the conditions of vulnerability to famine, regardless of whether exploitation is carried on by colonialism or natural governments. Moreover, market orientation of agricultural production does not only rationalize farming, it also promotes the organization of farmers and enables them to fight for their rights.

One of the primary issues that promoted agrarian protest in colonial Africa was the structure of the markets faced by the producers of cash crops. The commercialization of agriculture promoted significant economic gains, but, in some cases, the producers faced cartels that sought to appropriate these gains by engaging in price setting behaviour. Collusion on the part of the purchasers of cash crops furnished an incentive for the producers to combine and so achieve market power in an effort to increase their profits.[19]

In this context, colonial heritage means the continuation of exploitation of the rural masses even after independence. In order to establish the implicit assumption that colonialism is the origin of exploitation, however, one has to prove that exploitation did not exist in the pre-colonial period. Even if that were possible, it would still be necessary to show that colonialism must accept the responsibility for exploitation of which it is no more a direct agent nor a direct beneficiary. To continue to blame colonialism for famines that occur twenty or thirty years after independence is to abdicate responsibility and to make a sham of independence.[20]

As long as it is demonstrable that exploitation, poverty and famine are pre-and post-colonial facts, the intervening periods of colonialism can hardly serve as exploitations of famine.

Economic Exploitations

What we may call economic explanations of famine focus attention on the problems of food production and food distribution.

It may be necessary to state at the outset that problems of food production and food distribution are inherent in a subsistence production system, to which we attribute vulnerability to famine. But in and by themselves the problems of production and of distribution of food do not explain famine. These problems themselves as inherent parts of a subsistence production system call for exploitation.

Let us first dismiss the simple notion that land tenure is the cause of famine. The relationship between ownership of land and famine is very insignificant. In fact, the *awrajas* that are dominated by tenant cultivators are relatively better. Inequality in land distribution may become a factor of famine only in a subsistence production system, not in a commericialized farming system. This is the explanation for the fact that Illubabor, where about 70% of the farmers are tenants, is almost famine-free, whereas Tigray, where 80% are communal-individual owners, is famine-prone. Quite clearly insofar as famine is concerned, there are other factors that are more critical than land ownership. It may be granted, however, that, all other things remaining equal, tenants would have been even better off had they been owner cultivators.

In a given socio-economic system the distribution of the means of production as well as of goods and services follows certain rules. "Right can never be higher than the economic structure of society and its cultural development conditioned thereby."[21] Marx goes on to clarify the question of distribution in the following words:

> Any distribution whatever of the means of consumption is only a consequence of the distribution of the conditions of production themselves. The latter distribution, however, is a feature of the mode of production itself. . . . Bulgar socialism (and from it in turn a section of the democracy) has taken over from the bourgeois economists the consideration and treatment of distribution as independent of the mode of production and hence the presentation of socialism as turning principally on distribution.[22]

It is the use to which land, whether owned or rented, is put, and the incentives and disincetives to enlarge the farm size, as well as the nature and magnitude of exploitation, that loom large in famine. In certain instances, ownership of land has only a psychological value which is by no means unimportant. The concrete and real effect on the peasant is not less severe when he pays taxes to the government than when he pays rent to the landlord. In fact the burden is much heavier on the landowner than on the tenant, because the peasant landowner's obligations to the government and other claimants is usually much harder to waive than the tenant's obligation to the landlord. Maldistribution of land certainly does not explain famine in Ethiopia.

It is quite obvious that agricultural production is substantially reduced by various limitations imposed on input by the low level of scientific knowledge and technology, by archaic land tenure systems, and by the diminutive scale of operation of peasant farms.[23] Under such conditions, agricultural production is totally dependent on natural forces. Although it is, of course, evident that output is a function of input, we should at the same time remember that, in a subsistence production system, even the low output of peasants is further reduced by exploitation or by the claims of outsiders. This, in turn, directly or indirectly reduces input. The negative influence of the socio-economic and political forces has as much adverse effect on the peasant's output as on his capacity, both material and psychological, for input.

And yet one of the faint signs of hope for emerging out of a subsistence production system, the development of big commercial farms, is often presented as an explanation of famine.[24] It appears that in their attempt to find simple explanations for famine, many writers on this subject have identified commercial farming as exogenous to an essentially subsistence economy, and have jumped to the conclusion that this exogenous element is the cause of famine. In fact, some even maintain the untenable position of defending the scale of peasant farming.[25] They start from a certified fact that in many countries, including Ethiopia, productivity per unit of land is higher on smaller than on bigger farms. In attempting to understand the problem of famine and its relationship to peasant production, it makes very little sense to quote masses of data on productivity per unit of land. This is so general and obvious, and pertains to the developed countries as well, that it is not a peculiarity of under-developed economies. Farms in Western Europe or Japan have much higher productivity per unit of land than those in the United States. It is not enough, nor is it helpful, to state that yields per hectare are two, three, or four times those on bigger farms. The question is: How much is two, three, or four times in absolute terms?

A simple calculation will show that, for instance, in Ethiopia a farmer with five hectares, let us say, gets a yield of three quintals of *tef* per hectare, while a small peasant on only one-half of one hectare gets six quintals per hectare, the former has 15 quintals and the latter has only 3 at the end of the year. The yield per hectare of the small farmer is twice as much as that of the big farmer, but the total output of the big farmer is five times as much as that of the small farmer. Of course when one considers "farms" of even less than 0.5 hectare, the situation gets worse. For the small farmer the scrace factor is land, whereas for the big farmer it is labour, and so productivity of labour will be higher on the big farms while productivity of land will be higher on the small farms. In real terms, what is important is not the yields per unit of land, but *what is available to the peasant and his family* at the end of the harvest season, and after deducting the claims of outsiders. Such a view will place the peasant in the middle of a complex relationship with nature and society.

The undue idealization of the small peasant plots is a retrogressive view comparable to the well-known anthropologists' appeal "to leave the native alone". Colonial officials, too, made almost similar pleas; as a British Colonial officials said, "The surest test for the soundness of measures for the improvement of an uncivilized people is that they should be self-sufficient."[26] It is idle to believe that agricultural development can take place on miniscule farms where the majority of the population would remain permanently tied to the land. This is a nagging problem for those engaged in land reform and agricultural planning.

There is no doubt that peasant production has a very serious systemic problem. But the problem in itself alone cannot explain famine. Similarly, variations in the productivity of land and labour fail to explain famine, which is a malaise of the total subsistence production system with all its in-built disincentives and technical backwardness.

Objections to unequal distribution of land and more specifically to tenancy are more easily rationalized on social and political grounds than on economic ones. When equalization of land distribution is pushed to its logical conclusion, it becomes necessary to advocate garden farming, ignoring the advantages of scale. Such an advocacy of small peasant farms is essentially opposed to development.

Nor is there any guarantee that food production of small peasant farms will be adequate to prevent the threat of famine. It is not enough to state that all land should be under food crops, and no land should be under cash crops. It is also necessary to take into account the money value of alternative crops, the requirements for foreign exchange, and the possible gains for comparative advantage. Preoccupation with food production is one of the most serious problems of a subsistence production system. Opposition to high-value cash crops and advocacy of low-value food crops is, once more, a stand against development.[27]

Without the proper institutional arrangements and responsive as well as responsible government machinery, neither the distribution of land nor the distribution of food crop production will bear any result that can prevent famine. In other words, the allocation of all land resources to food production by itself cannot be an insurance against famine.

Neither does "inequality of food distribution" explain famine. This aspect of distribution is expressed as follows:

Since, historically speaking, most famines were preceded by crop failure due to natural disasters, it has seemed obvious to many that famines are caused by a "food shortage". This, however, is a fallacy. Food availability in a region or country does not depend on current local production alone. No region is a completely closed economy, and the possibility of trade exists. There are often stocks of food grains that are carried over from one year to another. A decline in current local production does not, therefore, automatically imply a decline in food availability.[28]

The argument boils down to the statement that crop failure in any one year does not lead to serious food shortages either because there are often stocks from previous years, or because it is always possible to import from outside. Let us assume for a moment that this is true. Food is available in the market. Does this mean that food is available to the starving people? It certainly is not.

This argument can in general be taken as valid for industrialized regions or countries, or for regions and countries where commercial agriculture is developed. But it is certainly invalid for subsistence producers who have neither the "stocks of food grains that are carried over from one year to another" nor the cash necessary to take advantage of "the possibility of trade". After stating that "in numerous instances in history, one crop failure in one part of a country led so large scale starvation deaths", the writer goes on to say, "The correct conclusion to be drawn from this is that in the course of a crop failure some people lose their access to food, and not that food as such becomes unavailable."[29] The point, presumably, is that food is available in general, but it is not available to those who have lost "access" to it, those who are starving to death. If the starving peasants had cash they would automatically have access to the available food. Peasants do not starve to death with cash in their pockets. It is effective demand that generates the mechanism of distribution, enabling people with the necessary cash power to command the acquisition of food supplies when they want them and where they want them at a price they are willing to pay. Such cash power, starving people do not possess. "The difficulty is a lack of buying power."[30]

Ultimately, however, the writer does accept that crop failure will "lead to starvation deaths in a pure peasant economy if there are peasant families (*i*) who survive at a level close to subsistence even in a normal year, and (*ii*) who do not possess exchangeable assets".[31] But this is lost in his final conclusion that famines are "caused not generally by absolute food shortages but by sudden increases in inequality of food distributions".[32] Perhaps another way of expressing these "sudden increases in inequality of food distribution" is sudden decrease in food production. Subsistence producers who suffer crop failure are more directly affected by loss of production rather than by the inequality in distribution, because they are outside the market or cash economy, and therefore, outside the mechanism of distribution. Even in the case of the commercial farmer, as Galbraith observes, in "both the markets in which he sells and those in which he buys, the individual farmer's market power in the typical case intrinsically nil".[33]

In Chapter Second we have already cited instances of grain rotting for lack of buyers at cheap subsidized prices. In Tigray, in 1959, food grains were available at abnormally cheap prices because grain merchants miscalculated in taking need for demand. People were dying of starvation, nevertheless. In 1973 there was a substantial stock of grain in Wello while the people were dying. The University relief team bought all the grain it distributed from Wello. The question is that in a famine situation where there is food grain in the market and where starving peasants have no cash, how do we transfer the food grain from the market to the starving peasants? In a country like Ethiopia, even free distribution of food grain entails an enormous cost.

Viewed globally, the distribution problem involves transfers of food from countries that have surplus to food deficit countries in form of trade or aid. Trade presupposes the availability of foreign exchange or easily exportable resources that can be converted into foreign currency. Food aid, on the other hand, is not governed by supply and demand but by either political association or humanitarian reasons, which really boils down to state pauperism supported by "a mighty myth".[34] Whether pauper states can demand the distribution of food in international system as a matter of moral right, or even of an economic right, is highly debatable. Moreover, even if it were possible to establish this right, it would not at all be helpful, because it only perpetuates state pauperism and erodes all hope for self-reliance.

To argue that the United States has the capacity to produce a much greater quantity of food than it does now neither establishes nor guarantees the flow of the surplus food from the United States to those countries that have a deficit. Political and trade barriers are facts that can hardly be ignored in any consideration of distribution of goods globally.

Demographic Explanations

One of the easiest and commonest explanations of famine is population growth. It is argued that as land resources remain constant at best or deteriorate considerably, and as agricultural technology remains primitive, while, as a consequence of these and other adverse factors, agricultural production proceeds at a snail's pace, population growth, mainly as a result of very high birth rate, soars much faster. One of the "Malthusian-type equilibrating mechanisms"[35] of such an imbalance between population growth and resources is famine. It is generally recommended to underdeveloped countries in particular that "the first requirement for dealing effectively with world hunger is to take measures to limit population growth".[36] Some writers state it even more forcefully: *"The only way* in which it makes sense to talk about solving the world food problem is to envision and achieve some degree of control over population numbers".[37]

Although it remains to be demonstrated, in the case of Ethiopia, it sounds reasonable to argue that in a subsistence production system where methods of farming have remained the same for generations, while the parcellation and fragmentation as well as the deterioration of farm land get progressively worse, population pressure may become one of the factors that make peasants vulnerable to famine. Such arguments assume that the cultivable land in a given country is fully and efficiently utilized, that alternative non-agricultural economic activities cannot develop, and that limiting population growth will solve the problem of poverty and famine. None of these assumptions can be taken as valid, at least for Ethiopia. There is yet plenty of scope for a more efficient utilization of the already cultivated land, and much more land can also be brought under cultivation.

There are areas in Ethiopia that, until recently, shielded by their remoteness and inaccessibility, remained relatively free from famine in spite of great population pressure on the land.[38] Statements that single out population growth as the cause of famine in Ethiopia have absolutely no ground. For instance, it is very difficult to substantiate a statement that "increase in human population is the most important single factor involved"[39] in famine in Ethiopia.

One of the major contributions of Susan George and Frances Moore Lappe is to annihilate the population growth myth. Fundamentally, the problem of famine is not necessarily and solely related to population growth. Many countries in Western Europe, Tsarist Russia and China have histories of famine. Now, in these same countries, in spite of much larger populations, famine, does not occur. This, certainly, is sufficient to exclude population growth as the cause of famine.

With a rational organization of society and with a rational management of resources, including people, the problem of famine can be eliminated. All other things remaining equal, population growth will certainly aggravate poverty and the problem of food supply in the rural areas of Ethiopia. But is it reasonable to assume that all other things will remain equal? Is it not at least equally reasonable to assume that abject poverty and widespread dissatisfaction will produce the necessary conditions for fundamental changes that can recharge and regenerate a stagnant society? We may pose the question differently: How resonable is it to assume that, all other things remaining equal, limiting population growth can improve rural life?

Cultural Explanations

In the context of Ethiopian culture, famine is not a natural calamity, nor does it have anything to do with society and its political and socio-economic system. Famine is an act of God. It is punishment to people who have sinned, and, of course, as often happens in life, what comes for the sinner does not spare the virtuous.[40] Famine is simply the price of sin and the victims accept it as such.

Since famine is totally taken out of the more or less manageable context of social relations, no human being or human institution can be held responsible for it. Likewise no human being or human institution can avert it. It is a very neat explanation that allows famine to be bearable.

The problem so neatly identified, the solution becomes neat, too: it is prayer for mercy and forgiveness. The Portugese priest, Alvarez, makes this point clear:

This country was entirely covered with locusts without wings, and they said these were the seed of those which had been there and destroyed the country, and they said that as soon as they had wings they would at once go and seek their country. I am silent as to the multitude of these without wings, because it is

not to be believed, and it is right that I should relate what more
I saw in this country. I saw men, women, and children seated
horror-struck amongst these locusts. I asked them: 'Why do you
stay there dying, why do you not kill these animals, and revenge
yourselves for the damage which their parents did you, and at
least the dead ones will do no further harm?' They answered that
they had not the heart to resist the plague which God gave them
for their sins.[41]

Alvarez, who does not have much respect for truth and who must
be read cautiously, also tells us that by prayer and "a requisition
and denunciation of excommunication" he set the locusts to flight,
so that the "next day in the morning there was not a single one
alive in the whole country".[42]

It is believed that one of the sins that invite the wrath of God is
working on the Sabbath and other Holy Days, of which in
Ethiopia there are some 240 annually. The observance of the
Sabbath and other Holy Days was not always voluntary. There was
social pressure, threat of excommunication, and even proclamations.
As recently as 1920 (E.C.), or 1928, there was the following proclamation:

Before this one there have been many proclamations forbidding
people to work on the Sabbath and other Holy Days excluded
from working days under pain of excommunication.

But now we realise that the wrath of God has not abated due
to your indulgence, against the excommunication [and proclamation, in working on the Holy Days, especially on the Sabbath.
From now on observe the Sabbath and other Holy Days. Do not
work on these days. Any person found working on these days
forbidden by both proclamation and excommunication shall be
punished.[43]

This is by no means a thinking of the past. In 1973, there was a
circular letter sent to all the *awrajas* and *weredas* of Wello requesting the admininstrators to urge the people to assemble and pray
for mercy every day "since there is no other solution except
repentance and prayer".[44]

Two points need to be made here, before leaving this subject.

First, the combined natural and socio-economic processes that precipitate famine are outside the Ethiopian cultural reality, taking reality to mean the understanding or the perception of the people at large. Perhaps the same idea is expressed by Alexander Spoehr when he says: "Man, to many peoples, is not set apart from nature but is part of a single order, combining man, nature, and the gods. When man utilizes the resources of nature, it is within the framework of this system of ideas."[45] No sharp separation exists between these three entities. Man is created in the image of God, and the rest of creation is for the enjoyment of man—there is no word for nature as an independent and dynamic force. In the Ethiopian cultural context, both man and the rest of creation come under the direct control of God, who manipulates them as he pleases.

The second point is that, since both government and people perceive famine as a special act of God, no mortal being is held responsible for it. For the government, therefore, this perception of famine has proved to be a convenient and successful means of disclaming its responsibility and obligation to avert famine. The same perception has enabled the people to accept suffering and death with peace and equanimity.

NOTES

[1]K. Walten, *The Arid Zones*, (London), p. 8.

[2]*Ibid.*, pp. 16-17.

[3]*Science and the Future of Arid Lands*, (UNESCO, Paris, 1960), p. 15.

[4]It is suggested, for instance, that in North Africa the Arid Region lies "between the isohyets of 100 to 400 millimeters," H.N. Le Houerou, in Harold E. Dregne ed, *Arid Lands in Transition*, (Washington D.C., 1970), p. 227. In Ethiopia, it is the 800 mm. isohyet that is taken often as the dividing line between the arid and humid regions.

[5]Benjamin Goodwin Wisner, Jr., *The Human Ecology of Drought in Eastern Kenya*, (Ph. D. Dissertation, Clark University, Worcester, 1977), p. 58.

[6]*Loc. cit.*

[7]Stephen Sandford, "Towards A Definition of Drought", in *Symposium on Drought in Botswana, op. cit.*, p. 34.

[8]W.C. Palmer, *Meteorological Drought*, (U.S. Weather Bureau, Washington D.C., 1965), p. 2.

[9]*Ibid.*, p. 3.

[10]See, for instance, Wisner, Jr., *op. cit.*, pp. 58-59.

[11]Stephen Sandford, *op. cit.*, p. 34.

[12]Frances Moore Lappe and George Collins with Cary Fowler, *Food First*,

Beyond the Myth of Scarcity, (A Ballantine Book, New York, 1979), p. 113. In this connection it may be instructive to read also pp. 99-117.

[13]Susan George, *op. cit.*, p. 15.

[14]Helge Kjekshus, *Ecology Control and Economic Development in East African History: The Case of Tanganyika, 1850-1950*, (Los Angels 1977), pp. 47-48. See also p. 142.

[15]Susan George, *op. cit.*, p. xvi, See also pp. 4-6.

[16]*Ibid.*, p. xviii.

[17]*Ibid.*, p. 31.

[18]R.H. Tawney, *The Acquisitive Society*, (A Harvest Book, New York, 1948), p. 49.

[19]Robert H. Bates, "The Commercialization of Agriculture and the Rise of Rural Political Protest in Black Africa" in Ed. Raymond F. Hophins, Donald J. Puchala, and Ross B. Talbot, eds., *Food, Politics, and Agricultural Development: Case Studies in the Public Policy of Rural Modernization*, (Westview Press, 1979), p. 231. This article is particularly useful to those who may want to have a general and balanced view of colonial agricultural policy.

[20]John Kenneth Galbraith, *Economic Development*, (Cambridge, Mass., 1965), p. 16. See also Gunnar Myrdal, *Economic Theory and Underdeveloped Regions*, (London, 1964), pp. 55-63.

[21]Karl Marx, *Selected Works*, *op. cit.*, Vol. III., p. 19.

[22]*Ibid.*, pp. 19-20.

[23]See Clifford M. Hardin, ed., *Overcoming World Hunger*, (Perspective Series, No. 2, NewYork, 1969).

[24]See sections by A.M. Hussein and Glynn Flood in A.M. Hussein, ed., *Drought and Famine in Ethiopia*, (African Environment Special Report 2, International African Institute, London, 1976). See also Peter Koehen, "Ethiopia: Famine, Food Production and Change in the Legal Order", *African Studies Review*, (Vol. XXII, No. 1, April, 1979).

[25]See Frances Moore Lappe *et al*, *op. cit.*, pp. 183-205, also Susan George, *op. cit.*, p. 15. For a detailed and thorough discussion on the subject, see R. Albert Berry and William R. Cline, *Agrarian Structure and Productivity in Developing Countries*, (Johns Hopkins University Press, Baltimore 1979).

[26]Quoted by Margery Perham, *The Colonial Reckoning: The Reith Lectures: 1961* (A Fontana Book, London, 1963), p. 92.

[27]See David Metcalf, *The Economics of Agriculture*, (A Penguin Book, London, 1969), pp. 72-84.

[28]Ajit Kumar Ghose, *Short-Term Changes in Income Distribution in Poor Agrarian Economies: A Study of Famine with Reference to the Indian Sub-Continent*, World Employment Programme Research, Working Paper, WEPI-6/ WP 28 (International Labour Office, Geneva, October, 1979), p. 2.

[29]*Ibid.*, p. 3.

[30]Clifford M. Hardin, ed., *op. cit.*, p. 82.

[31]*Ibid.*, p. 5.

[32]*Ibid.*, p. 34.

[33]John Kenneth Galbraith, *American Capitalism: The Concept of Countervailing Power*, (Penguin, London, 1956), p. 168.

[34]Clifford M. Hardin, ed., *op. cit.*, p. 83.

[35]Kimon Valaskakis *et al*, *The Conserver Society, A Workable Alternative for the Future*, (New York, 1979), p. 29.

[36]Clifford M. Hardin, ed., *Overcoming World Hunger*, (New York, 1969), p. 146.

[37]Clifford M. Hardin, ed., *op. cit.*, p. 65.

[38]See, for instance, R.T. Jackson and others, *Report of the Oxford University Expedition to the Gamu Highlands of Southern Ethiopia*, (Oxford, 1969, unpublished).

[39]RRC, *Drought and Rehabilitation in Wello and Tigray: Report of a Survey and Project Preparation Mission, October-November 1974*, (Addis Ababa, January, 1975), p. 22.

[40]An Ethiopian proverb.

[41]Father Francisco Alvarez, trans. Lord Stanley of Alderley, revised and edited C.B. Beckingham and G.W.B. Huntingford, *The Prester John of the Indies: Being the Narrative of the Protuguese Embassy to Ethiopia in 1920*, (Hakluyt Society, Cambridge, 1861), Vol. I., p. 136.

[42]*Ibid.*, pp. 133-134.

[43]The writer's translation from Amharic.

[44]17/7/65.

[45]Alexander Spoehr, "Cultural Differences in the Interpretation of Natural Resources", in *Man's Role in Changing the Face of the Earth*, (Chicago, 1962), p. 98.

Chapter Seven

The Analysis of Famines in Ethiopia: A New Explanation

It may be necessary to clarify some points at the outset. The area unit of investigation is the *awraja* or province, of which there are 102. These are second level administrative divisions, higher than the *wereda* or district, and lower than the *kifle hagher* or administrative region. The average area of an *awraja* is 12,000 square kms., and the average population is about 250,000.

Most *awrajas* have considerable internal variations in elevation, climate, vegetation cover, and soil fertility. As a result the productive capacities of various parts of an *awraja* may vary. A report on famine from any *awraja*, therefore, might not actually mean that the whole *awraja* was under famine. It might be that there were pockets of famine areas within the *awraja*, or conversely, there might be pockets of famine-free areas in a generally famine-stricken *awraja*. The criterion for determining whether or not an *awraja* had famine in a given year was that the famine information, in spite of extremely discouraging bureaucratic red tape, had reached the archives of the Ministry of Interior.

It may be recalled that unless the problem became extremely persistent and pressing the reports very often did not go beyond the *awraja* office, or at the most they might only reach the *kifle hagher* office. But when the reports of famine reached the Ministry of Interior in Addis Ababa, it was an almost clear sign that the problem was severe and persistent enough not to be ignored. Once famine information made the tortuous and uphill journey to the

Ministry of Interior, correspondence between the four administra-tive levels (*wereda, awraja, kifle hagher,* Ministry of Interior) con-tinued for months, and from the contents it is easy to determine not only the existence but also the magnitude of the problem of famine.

The methodology employed in this study for the analysis of famine begins with measureable dimensions of the problem. Using the available data on famine for a period of twenty years, 1958-1977, we shall now consider the three dimensions of famine in Ethiopia in very general terms.

The Temporal Dimension of Famine

The basic components of the temporal dimension of famine are the number and consecutivity of famine years. Taking the country as a whole, the most significant fact is that all the twenty years have been famine years. The average number of *awrajas* that suffered famine every year is 23.45. This means that, on the average, about 20% of the country was under famine in each of the 20 years. This at once demonstrates the magnitude and seriousness of the problem of famine in rural Ethiopia. The number of *awrajas* under a famine in each year is shown in Table XIII.

Quite obviously the worst famine years are 1973-1975, during which more than 50 *awrajas* were under famine in spite of unprece-dented national and international relief aid. Although the number of famine-stricken *awrajas* in 1966 had risen to 60, it dropped to only 10 in the following year. From 1965 to 1968 famine persisted only in the most severely affected *awrajas* while most seem to have recover-ed after only one year of famine. The 1966 famine had affected the normally famine free *awrajas* in south-central and western parts of the country. These are relatively more commercialized, which may be the reason why famine did not persist.

The two best years are 1964 and 1969, with only five and four *awrajas* under famine, respectively.

During the period under consideration, two *awrajas* have had eight consecutive years of famine, one *awraja* had six, and ten *awrajas* had five consecutive years of famine.

Another aspect of the temporal dimension of famine is its cumu-lative character. If we divide the twenty years into five four-year periods (Table XV), we observe this cumulative effect of famine rather emphatically. (*Figure 6*). The number of *awraja* famine years

TABLE XIII

NUMBER OF *Awrajas* UNDER FAMINE IN EACH YEAR, 1958-1977

Year: 19	58	59	60	61	62	63	64	65	66	67	68	69	70	71	72	73	74	75	76	77	Total
Famine *awrajas*	12	21	14	11	12	10	5	25	60	10	15	4	28	12	13	56	61	53	21	26	469
% Total *awrajas*	11.8	20.6	13.7	10.8	11.8	9.8	4.9	24.5	58.8	9.8	14.7	3.9	27.4	11.8	12.7	54.7	59.8	52.0	20.6	25.5	
Kind of Famine	R	R	R	R	R	R	L	R	N	R	R	L	R	L	L	L	N	N	R	R	

L=Local; R=Regional; N=National.

rises from 58 in Period I to 161 in Period V. Famine apparently leaves not merely a scar but an exposed scar that reduces resistance

FAMINE: CUMULATIVE NUMBER OF AWRAJAS UNDER FAMINE

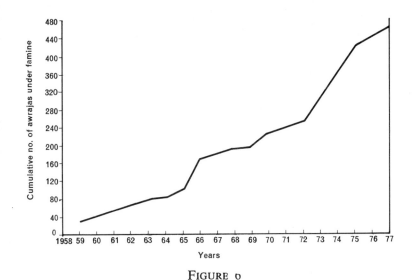

FIGURE ɒ

TABLE XIV
FREQUENCY OF FAMINE,
1958-1977

	Famine Years													Total
Frequency	0	1	2	3	4	5	6	7	8	9	10	11	12	13	91
No. awrajas	7	11	10	12	8	18	10	9	6	5	4	1	0	1	102

TABLE XV
NUMBER OF *Awrajas* UNDER FAMINE IN FOUR-YEAR PERIODS
1958-1977

Periods	I	II	III	IV	V
Years: 19—	58-61	62-65	66-69	70-73	74-77
Famine *awarajas*	58	52	89	109	191
Index period I=100%	100	89.6	153.4	189.9	277.6

to future risks. Although the time span is rather short for any firm conclusion, it is nevertheless noteworthy that some cyclical movement of famine is detectable. While the trend is generally upward, four years of falling famine and four years of rising famine seem to follow each other; a four-year cycle of famine appears to be indicated (*Figure 7*). It may be enlightening to compare the export and import of cereals with the number of famine *awrajas* for each year (*Figure 8*).

The Spatial Dimension of Famine

Within the twenty years under consideration the movement and expansion of famine over Ethiopia is astounding. Out of the 102 *awrajas* in the country, only seven did not experience any famine. The *awrajas* that are free form a narrow belt running mainly from Gonder to Kefa. The *awrajas* that have had no famine together with those that had only one famine each form a more or less continuous area—from Gonder through Gojjam and Wellega to Kefa, northern Sidamo, and northern Gamo Gofa, with some *awrajas* in Bale, Arsi, and Harerghe. The Ethiopian Rift Valley, with the exception of the Middle Awash Valley, and the adjoining highlands as well as the lowlands in the north, west, and south and southeast constitute the regions of famine.

Table XVI shows the yearly expansion of famine. The initial number of *awrajas* under famine in 1958 is 12. Then in each of most of the subsequent 19 years, one or more *new awrajas* fell under famine. There were only three years (1967, 1968 and 1971) during which famine did not conquer any new *awraja*. Quite clearly in 1965 and 1966 famine brought under its grinding teeth the largest number of new *awrajas*, 17 and 18 respectively. On the

TABLE XVI
NUMBER OF *Awarajas* UNDER FAMINE IN EACH YEAR,
1958-1977

Year: 19-	58	59	60	61	62	63	64	65	66	67	68	69	70	71	72	73	74	75	76	77
Famine *awrajas* Cumulative	12	23	29	31	41	45	46	63	81	81	81	82	87	87	88	89	90	91	94	95
New famine *awrajas*, No.	12	11	6	2	10	4	1	17	18	0	0	1	5	0	1	1	1	1	3	1

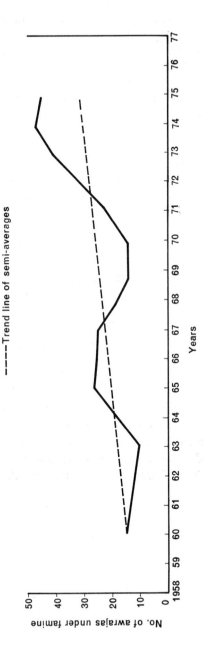

FOUR-YEAR MOVING AVERAGES AND SEMI-AVERAGE TREND LINE

—— Four-year moving averages (centred)
----- Trend line of semi-averages

No. of awrajas under famine

Years

FIGURE 7

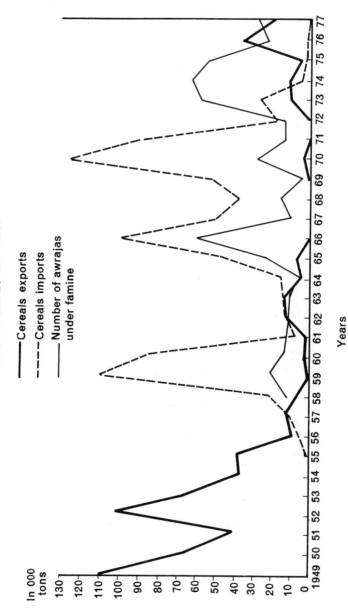

EXPORT AND IMPORT OF CEREALS, 1949—1975 AND FAMINE, 1958—1977

Cereals exports
Cereals imports
Number of awrajas under famine

In 000 tons

Years

FIGURE 8

average four new *awrajas* were falling under famine each year. It is evident, too, that by the end of 1966 already 81 of the 102 *awrajas* had come under the grip of famine. We may therefore note with

**DIAGRAM TO ILLUSTRATE THE EFFECT
OF SPATIAL EXTENSION (DIMENSION) OF FAMINE**

Local famine

Regional famine

National famine

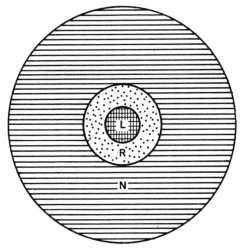

All other things remaining equal,
Potential supply area for L is R + N
Potential supply area for R is N
Potential supply area for N is external

As the famine area expands the potential
demand increases while the potential supply
area diminishes.

FIGURE 9

sorrow that, in the following twelve years, famine, for the most part, was merely revisiting familiar areas, but with greater ferocity. The total number of *awrajas* with famine experience rises to 95 by 1977 (*Figure 9*).

Perhaps the most important aspect of the spatial dimension of famine is the relative extent of area or number of *awrajas* in a particular year. This aspect of the spatial dimension of famine enables us to assess the destructive capacity of famine in a given year. The larger the contiguous area under famine, the greater the destructive capacity of famine, discounting relief aid which, so far at any rate, has invariably come too late. In a national famine, therefore, the damage wrought by famine stands at the very extreme end of a scale, and at the other extreme we have local famine, under which the destructive capacity of famine is limited to a rather small area. In between the national and local famine, somewhat nearer to the local famine than to the national, we find regional famine. For local famine all other things being equal, the potential supply area in relation to the potential demand (need) is most extensive, whereas for national famine, on the contrary, it is least extensive. In other words, as the famine area expands, the area of potential demand (need) increases, while the potential supply area diminishes. (See *Figure 10*.)

In Eihiopia, there have been four national famines, twelve regional famines and four local famines in the twenty years. A pattern emerges, if we divide the twenty years into two halves: the first half has only one local famine, eight regional famines, and only one national famine; the second half, on the other hand, has three local famines, four regional famines, and three national famines. It is clear, therefore, that in the second half of the period, famine had become entrenched and had expanded over most of the country. Here again we see signs of the cumulative and the incapacitating effect of famine.

The Demographic Dimension of Famine

We study famine because we witness the misery and suffering of human beings, and feel, in a very remote way, their agony and their helpless death. The demographic dimesion, that is the effect of famine on people, is therefore central. But in a country like Ethiopia, where famine deaths have never been carefully recorded and where pertinent data are very fragmentary and mostly no more than illiterate guesswork, the assessment of the demographic dimension of famine confronts us with grave difficulties.

Ideally we should have accurate data on the populations of each *awraja*, the rate of population growth, famine mortality and

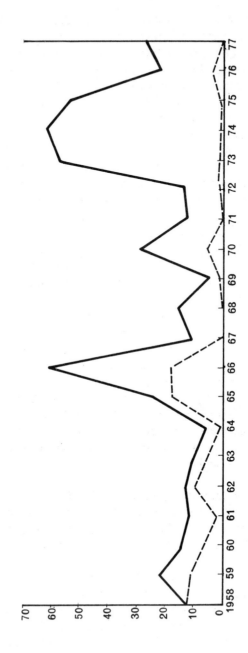

TOTAL AND NEW FAMINE AWRAJAS 1958—1977

——— Total awrajas under famine

- - - - New awrajas under famine

FIGURE 10

emigration rate, and changes in the age and sex structure and composition of the population. With such data it would have been relatively easy to assess the demographic dimension of famine. But we have no such data. In such circumstances, it is still necessary to devise a rough index for measuring the demographic dimension of famine, as we shall presently see.

The March of Famine

During the twenty years under review, the annual march or movement of famine shows an irregular but a clearly discernible pattern. Famine seems to follow a path of least resistance and, as long as conditions remain more or less the same, as time goes on more and more *awrajas* lose their resistance to famine.

The scar left by famine forms a belt covering the north-eastern, eastern, and southern parts of the country. Famine has been generally moving clockwise and forming a spiral. The regional famine of Tigray, in 1958, spreads northward into Eritrea in 1959. Within the twenty-year period, therefore, we take Tigray and Eritrea as the original areas of famine. In the following two years, 1960 and 1961, the ugly claws of famine stretch southward to grip the Middle Awash Valley and the southeastern low lands Harerghe and Bale. In 1962 and 1963 famine moves westward through Sidamo into Gamo Gofa, then extending northward to southwestern Kefa, eastern Illubabor, western Wellega, and western Gojjam. This means that in the first six years, most of the *awrajas* along the eastern, southern, and western borders of the country have already fallen under famine.

In 1964 and 1965 famine penetrates into the central parts of the country to form a second inner spiral. This second belt of casualty starts from Wello, immediately south of Tigray, and stretches southward through eastern Sewa into Arsi and then westward into Kafa, Illubabor and Wellega. The last *awrajas* to fall under famine in 1975, 1976, and 1977 are Limu in Kefa, Arjo in Wellega, Bahir Dar in Gojjam, Debre Tabor in Gonder, and Chebo and Guraghe in Shewa. These *awrajas* are in the region which, during the period of study, has remained relatively more resistant to famine.

The march of famine in space and time seems to reveal two points. First, the most vulnerable *awrajas* seem the first to succumb to the stress and strain of the vicissitudes that introduce famine. Second, under prevailing conditions, and given time, the trend suggests that all the *awrajas* are potentially vulnerable to famine. It may, in addition, be stated that, if conditions remain the same or get worse, every famine leaves a scar that aggravates vulnerability to future famine (See *Figure 11*).

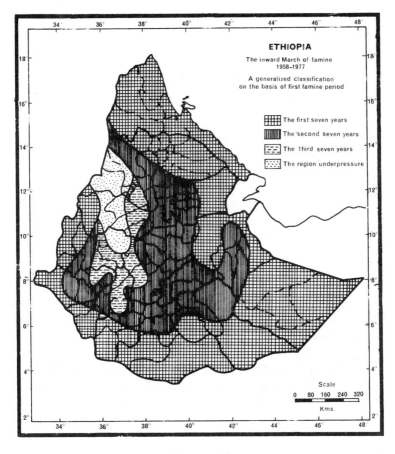

ETHIOPIA

The inward March of famine
1958-1977

A generalized classification
on the basis of first famine period

The first seven years

The second seven years

The third seven years

The region underpressure

Scale

0 80 160 240 320

Kms.

FIGURE 11

Quantification

So far we have attempted to show that famine cannot be explained away by the vagaries of nature alone, nor by one or two factors of the socio-economic and political system. We have rejected the various conventional explanations of famine. Instead, we have insisted that amine is a product of a subsistence production system.

We believe that our argument will be strengthened if we quantify famine, the quality of the physical environment, subsistence level, farm commercialization, and level of development. The methodology employed for quantifying these five variables and the formulation of indexes which measure the relative position of each *awraja* is described below.

A. *Measurement of Famine*

(i) *Temporal Intensity*. The frequency and persistence of famine may be expressed in terms of its temporal dimension. The central aspect of the temporal dimension of famine is the consecutivity of famine years. It may be useful to define some terms first. Consecutivity expresses the uninterrupted succession of famine years. By famine period we mean a set of famine year or years which may be one isolated famine year, or a number of consecutive famine years. The length of the famine period depends on consecutivity, i.e. on the number of consecutive famine years.

Within the ith famine period, the j^{h} famine year is assigned a value, c_{ij}. If it is an isolated famine year or if it is the first famine year of a consecutive set, it is given a value of one. that is $c_{ij}=1$. We make the assumption that the intensity of famine increases with consecutivity. Although it is possible to argue for a geometrical progression, an arithmetic progression with a common difference of one is sufficient for the purpose of this study, to measure the increase of the intensity of famine. Consequently, c_{i_2}, the value of intensity for the second year of the ith period is 2; and in general for the j^{h} year of the ith period $c_{ij}=j$. Thus c_{ij} being so defined, if the ith famine period has x_i consecutive years of famine for a specific *awraja*, the measure of intensity for the ith period, c_i, is defined by:

$$c_i = \sum_{j=1}^{x_i} c_{ij} = \sum_{j=1}^{x_i} j$$

This means that c_i stands for the sum of values of intensity assigned for each year in that famine period. But as we have noted above, the length of the famine period varies, and so also does the length of the famine free period. Now, if n_i is the number of famine years in that period plus the number of famine-free years before and after it, and x_i stands for the number of famine years in the ith period, the temporal intensity, t_i for the ith famine period is given the value of

$$t_i = \frac{n_i c_i}{n_i - x_i}.$$

It should be noted that the ratio $\dfrac{}{n_i - x_i}$ increases with x_i and decreases with n_i. Hence multiplying this ratio by the measure of famine intensity for that period should be a reasonable measure of temporal intensity for that period.

To get the temporal intensity of famine for an *awraja* we add the values of intensity for all the famine periods of that *awraja*. This is done because it is maintained that intensity has an additive or cumulative effect through the whole time-span of the study for a given *awraja*. Hence:

$$T = \Sigma t_i,$$

i going through the number of famine periods for that *awroja*. Then T is transformed into standard scores to give us the temporal index (TI_z) as follows:

$$TI_z = \frac{T - \bar{T}}{T_s}$$

(*ii*) *Spatial Intensity.* One of the dimensions of famine is its spatial extension. In order to measure the intensity of the spatial dimension of famine for the kth year, we compute the ratio of the number of *awrajas* under famine to the total number of *awrajas* in the country. The ratio for the kth year is assigned to each *awraja* under famine that year. In other words, all *awrajas* under famine in the kth year will have the same ratio. In the same manner, the ratio is computed for all *awrajas* that are under each year. All *awrajas* that are famine-free in any year are assigned a value of 0. The sum of these ratios for each *awraja* under famine measures the spatial intensity (S) of famine for the whole twenty-year period, as follows:

$$S = \sum_{k=1}^{20} \frac{N_k}{102}$$

where $N_k =$ the number of *awrajas* under famine in the kth year, and 102 represents the total number of *awrajas* in the country. Finally S is transformed into standard scores to give us the spatial intensity index (SI_z) of famine. That is:

$$SI_z = \frac{S - \bar{S}}{S_s}$$

(*iii*) *Demographic Intensity.* The third and final measure of intensity of famine is in terms of population. If an *awraja* has famine in the rth year, then demographic ratio of r_k is determined by the ratio of the total rural population of all *awrajas* under famine that year to the rural population of the country. That is r_k=rural population of *awrajas* under famine in the kth year over the total rural population of the country. This means that all *awrajas* under famine in the kth year will have the same demographic ratio, r_k. In the same manner, for each year the demographic ratio is computed for those *awrajas* that are under famine. All those *awrajas* that are famine-free in any year are given a demographic ratio of 0.

Then, for each *awraja*, the demographic intensity (*D*) is defined to be the sum of the yearly demographic ratios of the *awrajas*. That is

$$D = \sum_{k=1}^{20} r_k$$

D is then transformed into standard scores to yield the final demographic index (*DIz*):

$$DI_z = \frac{D - \bar{D}}{D_s}$$

(*iv*) *The Famine Index.* The famine index is computed by first taking the mean of the three intensities described above for each *awraja*, as follows:

$$F = \frac{TI_z + SI_z + DI_z}{3}$$

Then, the results are transformed into standard scores to get the famine index (*FIz*):

$$FI_z = \frac{E - F}{F_s}$$

(See *Figure 12*).

B. *Measurement of Subsistence Level*

The calculation of the subsistence level index (SLI) involves a very laborious process. It starts with the calculation of the production of the various crops in each *awraja* by multiplying the number of hectares under each crop in each *awraja* by the national average yield per hectare. Then, using the 1970 prices, all crops are changed into their sorghum equivalents. Similarly all domestic animals in

Tropical Bovine Unit (TBU)[1] are changed into their sorghum equivalents. Then, in order to capture the variations in physical productivity, the sum of all sorghum equivalent for each *awraja* is multiplied by soil rating. The sum of all sorghum equivalents for

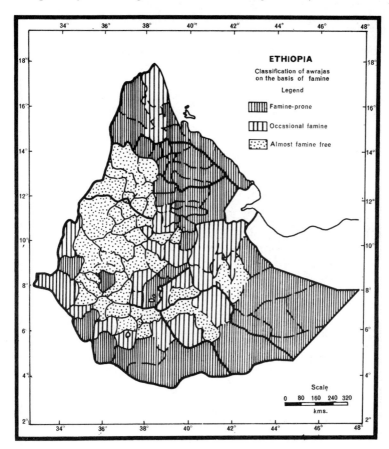

FIGURE 12

each *awraja* is then divided by the number of rural households. The share of sorghum equivalent of each household is divided by five to get the share per person. In other words:

$$Y = \frac{S(G_q + T_q)}{5H}$$

where Y=sorghum equivalent per person, G_q=the sorghum equivalent of all crops, T_q=the sorghum equivalent of all domestic animals, S=*awraja* soil rating, H=rural households, and 5 is the average size of a rural household. Then the subsistence level index (SLI_z) in standardized units will be

$$SLI_z = \frac{Y - \overline{Y}}{Y_s}.$$

(See *Figure 13*).

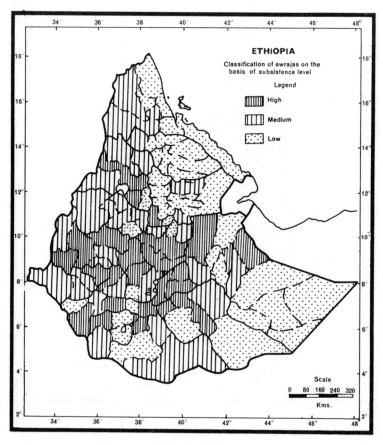

FIGURE 13

C. *Measurement of Farm Commercialization*

For calculating the farm commercialization index (*CI*), we have taken the percentages that each *awraja* has out of the total for the country as a whole in the following: land under commercial crops, urban population, number of marketplaces. In addition, we have

taken the average farm size for each *awraja*. Each of the four variables was first transformed into standard scores. Then the arithmetic
mean of the standard scores was computed for each *awraja* as
follows:

$$M = \frac{a_z + b_z + c_z + d_z}{4},$$

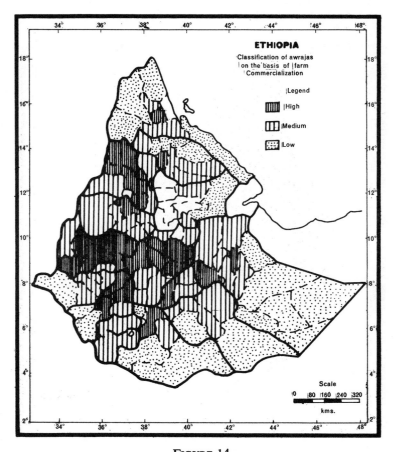

FIGURE 14

where $M =$ the mean, $a =$ the percentage of land under commercial
crops, $b =$ the percentage of urban population, $c =$ the percentage
of market places, and $d =$ the size of cultivated land, and where all
the four values are in standardized units. Finally the result is once

again transformed into a standardized variable. That is,

$$CI_z = \frac{M - \overline{M}}{M_s}$$

(See *Figure 14* on p. 163)

D. *Measurement of Environmental Quality*

In order to assess the relative quality of the physical environment with an environmental quality index (EQI), we have taken five

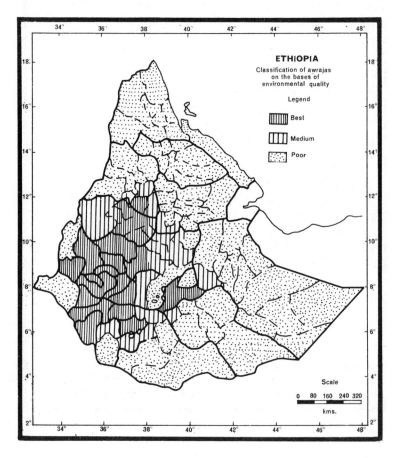

FIGURE 15

variables for each *awraja*: the ratio of mean annual rainfall to the mean annual temperature, the number of rainy days over 120, the quotient of 100 divided by the coefficient of variation of annual rainfall, (in order to reverse the direction and to reduce the numbers to facilitate calculation), soil rating, and proportion of cultivable land in relation to total area. Each of the five variables was transformed into standard scores. Then the arithmetic mean was computed as follows:

$$w = \frac{m_z + u_z + t_z + s_z + l_z}{5},$$

where w = the arithmetic mean, m = the ratio of rainfall to temperature, u = the proportion of rainy days, t = the transformed coefficient of variation of annual rainfall, s = soil rating out of ten, and l = the proportion of cultivable land out of total area—all in standard scores. Then once again, the means are changed into standard scores, so that

$$EQI_z = \frac{w - \overline{w}}{w_s}$$

(See *Figure 15* on p. 164)

E. *Measurement of Development*

In order to have a rough idea of the relative level of development of each *awraja*, scores of 0 or 1 are given depending on the absence (0) or presence (1) of the following 13 selected indicators of development: all-weather road, rail-road, airport, telephone, post office, bank, filling station, hospital, electricity, pipe water, secondary school, large scale commercial farming, industry. Then these scores are added to yield T, which is the total number of scores for each *awraja*. Then the development index (DI) is transformed into a standardized variable as follows:

$$DI_z = \frac{T - \overline{T}}{T_z}$$

(See *Figure 16* on p. 166)

All the five indexes computed for each *awraja*, as described above, are shown in Table XX at the end of this chapter.

Hypothesis Testing

The hypothesis which forms the basis of this study, twenty years of famine in rural Ethiopia, may be restated: subsistence rather than commercial farming is the condition of famine in rural Ethiopia. In other words, famine in rural Ethiopia is associated more with production for mere subsistence rather than with commercialized production. We will now test the association between famine, subsistence level, farm commercialization, environmental quality, and so-called development, in pairs. Our main interest, however, is the association or non-association between famine and subsistence level, and between famine and farm commercialization

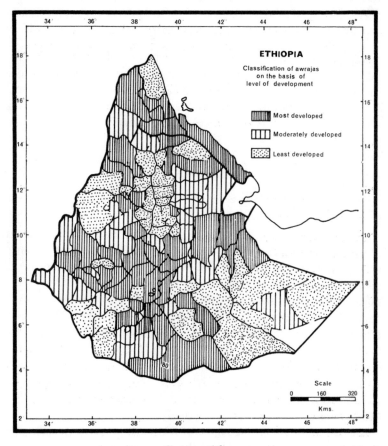

FIGURE 16

as well as between subsistence level and farm commercialization. The variables on environmental quality and on development are included for the purpose of testing the assumed greater dependence of subsistence producers on the natural environment rather than on the so-called development.

The methodology used to test the association between the five variables, two at a time, is the chi-square test of independence with a three-by-three contingency table.[2] A very determined effort is made to partition the *awrajas* into three classes on the basis of each of the five indexes. For all the indexes the cut-off point is $+0.44$ and -0.40.

We shall first conduct the test of independence between famine and subsistence level. The three-way classification on the basis of the famine index and the subsistence level index is shown below, in Table XVII.

TABLE XVII
THREE-BY-THREE CONTINGENCY TABLE:
Famine (F) and Subsistence (S)

	F_1	F_2	F_3	Total
S_1	5	9	15	29
S_2	8	8	16	32
S_3	24	11	6	41
Total	37	28	37	102

The competing hypotheses under test are

H_0: Famine and Subsistence level are independent.

H_1: H_0 is not true.

The test statistic we use is

$$X^2 = \sum \frac{(f_o - f_t)^2}{f_t}$$

where f_o = observed frequency, and f_t = theoretical frequency. The critical value of chi-square given at 0.01 level of significance for four degrees of freedom is 13.28. Since our calculated value of chi-square. 31.76, is very much in excess of the one given, we reject the null hypothesis and affirm our original hypothesis of close association between famine and subsistence level.

In order to measure the degree of relationship between each pair of the five indexes, we have used the following statistic:

Coefficient of Association (C.A.) $= \sqrt{\dfrac{X^2}{n + X^2}}$

But, since the coefficient of association does not indicate the direction of relationship, we have a supplementary coefficient of correlation from standard scores based on the following statistic:

$$C.C. = \frac{\Sigma(z_1 z_2)}{n}$$

TABLE XVIII

CALCULATION OF CHI-SQUARE FOR FAMINE AND SUBSISTENCE

f_0	f_t	$f_0 - f_t$	$(f_0 - f_t)^2$	$\dfrac{(f_0 - f_t)^2}{f_t}$
5	10.52	−5.52	30.47	2.90
8	7.96	0.04	0.00	0.00
24	10.52	13.48	181.71	17.27
9	11.61	−2.61	6.81	0.59
8	8.78	−0.78	0.61	0.07
11	11.61	−0.61	0.37	0.03
15	14.87	0.13	0.02	0.00
16	11.26	4.47	22.47	2.00
6	14.87	−8.87	78.68	5.29
120.00	102.00			28.15

Exactly similar calculations of chi-squares and coefficients of association and of correlation are calculated for each of the following combinations:

1. Famine (F) and farm commercialization (C)
2. Famine and the quality of the environment (E)
3. Famine and level of development (D)
4. Subsistence level (S) and farm commercialization
5. Subsistence level and the quality of the environment
6. Subsistence level and level of development
7. Farm commercialization and level of development
8. Farm commercialization and quality of environment
9. Level of development and quality of environment

The results for these combinations are summarized in Table XIX.
At 0.01 level of significance, the null hypothesis of independence is confirmed by the evidence only for famine and development, and for environmental quality and development. In all the other combinations, the null hypothesis is rejected with a level of confidence greater than 99%. To be more specific, for each of the combinations—famine and subsistence level, famine and farm commercialization, famine and environmental quality, subsistence level and farm commercialization, subsistence level and environmental quality,

TABLE XIX

CHI-SQUARES, COEFFICIENTS OF ASSOCIATION AND
OF CORRELATION FOR 10 COMBINATIONS

Combination	X^2	C.A.	C.C.
FxS	28.15	0.4651	—0.3343
FxC	63.40	0.6191	—0.3857
FxE	54.59	0.5904	—0.6040
FxD	2.27	0.1475	—0.0896
SxC	55.68	0.5942	0.5975
SxE	48.81	0.5689	0.5386
SxD	17.03	0.3783	0-2497
CxD	49.06	0.5699	0.4678
CxE	92.53	0.6897	0.4024
DxE	2.02	0.1394	0.0265

subsistence level and development farm commercialization and environmental quality and farm commercialization and development —the null hypothesis of independence is rejected with more than 99% confidence.

The fact that famine is fairly well but negatively associated with level of subsistence, farm commercialization, and environmental quality clearly confirms the original hypothesis that famine is inseparably connected with a subsistence production system. In other words, the results support our hypothesis that a system in which the majority of peasants are totally dependent on the physical environment and on their backward methods of production, and in which the socio-economic and political forces persist in incapacitating the productive potential of peasants by incessant oppression and exploitation is a condition for vulnerability to famine.

A higher level of subsistence suggests the availability of a greater surplus either for the market or for future use. Therefore, the higher the level of subsistence, the less will be the probability of famine. Similarly, a higher level of farm commercialization suggests a higher degree of market transactions and the availability of relatively more cash both for present and future use. Therefore, a higher level of farm commercialization means a lesser probability of famine. A higher level of subsistence means surplus production and, in turn, the type and magnitude of the surplus determines the level of farm commercialization. As the level of subsistence rises, the level of farm commercialization also rises, while the probability of famine falls.

Inversely, the probability of famine rises as the levels of subsistence and of farm commercialization fall.

The fact that level of subsistence and farm commercialization are very closely and positively related further confirms our basic argument that an almost exclusive production for subsistence is one of the necessary conditions for famine. Farm production that approximates to bare subsistence level, together with the irreducible claims of outsiders, ensures stagnation or even deterioration of both the quality of peasant life and the quality of the physical environment. This is the condition that creates vulnerability to famine.

How do we explain the fact that, strangely enough, the null hypothesis is confirmed for famine and development, and for the environmental quality and development? It is certainly tempting to conclude that the so-called development is utterly irrelevant to the basic problems of the country. It does seem to indicate that the identification of problems, the setting of priorities and implementation of projects and plans, does take into account the real and felt needs of the people nor the capabilities of the physical environment.

That farm commercialization is positively related to development is to be expected, because commercialization is normally an aspect of development. It may be noted, however, that in Ethiopia it is development that is an aspect of commercialization. In other words, farm commercialization precedes the various other indicators of development. Those who have vested interests in farm commercialization also have the power to influence the distribution of the development indicators.

It is also interesting to note that, although farm commercialization is positively related to both environmental quality and to development, development and environmental quality are hardly related. Taking this fact at its face value may suggest that development, as a manifestation of the assertion of man's technological advancement and his ability to command capital, provides him with the power to be almost independent of the constraints of the physical environment. In fact, the truth may be that the development policy failed to take into account the cost of overcoming the constraints of the physical environment and the ultimate goal of genuine development which is the well-being of people. Development was not directed at people, but rather at exploitable land.

On the other hand, farm commercialization is cost conscious. This is evident from the much greater relationship between farm

TABLE XX
INDEXES

No.	Name of Awrajas	FI	SI	CI	EI	DI
1.	Arba Gugu	0.18	1.38	0.35	0.38	$\overline{0}$.05
2.	Chilalo	$\overline{0}$.20	2.41	2.22	0.85	$\overline{1}$.09
3.	Ticho	$\overline{1}$.11	0.67	0.31	0.79	$\overline{0}$.91
4.	Dello	$\overline{0}$.37	$\overline{0}$.51	$\overline{0}$.76	$\overline{0}$.62	$\overline{1}$.20
5.	Ghenale	$\overline{1}$.02	1.23	0.16	0.45	$\overline{0}$.34
6.	Mendeyyo	$\overline{0}$.62	0.96	0.34	$\overline{0}$.13	0.81
7.	Wabe	$\overline{0}$.15	0.18	$\overline{0}$.15	$\overline{0}$.80	$\overline{0}$.91
8.	Elkerre	3.75	$\overline{0}$.77	$\overline{1}$.13	$\overline{1}$.48	$\overline{1}$.77
9.	Chilga	$\overline{1}$.51	0.42	0.01	0.02	$\overline{0}$.91
10.	Debre-Tabor	$\overline{0}$.88	0.98	0.70	0.17	$\overline{1}$.34
11.	Gayint	$\overline{0}$.50	$\overline{0}$.53	$\overline{0}$.42	0.70	$\overline{0}$.91
12.	Gonder	$\overline{1}$.51	0.82	1.07	0.13	1.66
13.	Libbo	$\overline{1}$.05	2.24	0.51	0.74	$\overline{1}$.20
14.	Semen	$\overline{0}$.51	$\overline{0}$.13	0.15	$\overline{0}$.03	$\overline{0}$.63
15.	Weghera	$\overline{0}$.64	0.05	0.66	$\overline{0}$.20	$\overline{0}$.52
16.	Gardulla	$\overline{0}$.07	$\overline{0}$.96	$\overline{0}$.36	0.60	$\overline{0}$.34
17.	Gheleb and Hamer Bakko	0.93	$\overline{0}$.39	$\overline{0}$.51	$\overline{0}$.10	$\overline{0}$.91
18.	Gamo	$\overline{0}$.64	$\overline{0}$.98	$\overline{0}$.27	0.89	1.09
19.	Gofa	$\overline{0}$.18	0.44	0.10	0.77	$\overline{1}$.49
20.	Aghew-Midir	$\overline{1}$.51	$\overline{0}$.29	$\overline{0}$.35	0.75	$\overline{0}$.34
21.	Bahir-Dar	$\overline{1}$.34	$\overline{0}$.13	1.22	1.14	0.81
22.	Bichena	$\overline{0}$.41	0.32	$\overline{0}$.12	0.74	$\overline{0}$.63
23.	Qolla-Dega Damot	$\overline{1}$.51	$\overline{0}$.13	0.10	1.12	$\overline{0}$.23
24.	Debre-Marqos	$\overline{0}$.74	$\overline{0}$.52	0.23	0.93	0.81
25.	Metekkil	$\overline{0}$.88	0.23	0.23	0.65	$\overline{1}$.20
26.	Mota	$\overline{0}$.97	$\overline{0}$.27	$\overline{0}$.35	0.87	$\overline{1}$.20
27.	Chercher, Adal and Garra Gurracha	0.15	0.77	0.30	$\overline{1}$.25	1.09
28.	Habro	$\overline{0}$.14	0.39	1.29	0.47	$\overline{0}$.05
29.	Dire-Dawa, Isa and Gurgura	$\overline{0}$.14	$\overline{0}$.62	0.0	$\overline{1}$.37	1.95
30.	Garamulleta	$\overline{0}$.59	$\overline{0}$.61	$\overline{0}$.30	$\overline{0}$.53	$\overline{0}$.91
31.	Gursum	$\overline{1}$.05	$\overline{0}$.21	$\overline{0}$.45	$\overline{0}$.80	$\overline{0}$.91
32.	Harer	$\overline{0}$.27	0.74	1.39	$\overline{0}$.35	1.09
33.	Weberra	0.10	$\overline{0}$.50	$\overline{0}$.35	0.05	$\overline{0}$.34
34.	Jijiga	0.59	0.81	$\overline{0}$.80	$\overline{0}$.99	1.09
35.	Degahabur	0.45	$\overline{0}$.48	$\overline{1}$.05	$\overline{1}$.29	$\overline{1}$.77
36.	Qebrri Deharre	0.45	$\overline{1}$.44	$\overline{1}$.09	$\overline{1}$.77	$\overline{0}$.34
37.	Warder	0.45	1.71	1.05	$\overline{2}$.07	$\overline{1}$.77
38.	Qellaffo	0.45	$\overline{0}$.78	$\overline{0}$.97	$\overline{1}$.61	$\overline{1}$.49
39.	Gode	0.45	$\overline{1}$.51	$\overline{1}$.05	$\overline{1}$.71	$\overline{0}$.91
40.	Bunno-Beddelle	0.52	0.79	0.13	1.67	0.52
41.	Gambella	0.01	$\overline{0}$.42	$\overline{0}$.57	0.41	0.23

No.	Name of Awrajas	EI	SI	CI	EI	DI
42.	Sor and Ghebba	$\bar{1}.29$	1.14	$\bar{0}.15$	1.80	.23
43.	Gore	$\bar{1}.29$	0.07	$\bar{0}.12$	1.44	0.52
44.	Mocha	$\bar{1}.11$	0.03	$\bar{0}.48$	1.38	$\bar{0}.34$
45.	Ghimira	$\bar{0}.21$	$\bar{0}.69$	$\bar{0}.76$	1.27	$\bar{0}.63$
46.	Jimma	$\bar{0}.85$	0.34	0.70	1.21	1.66
47.	Kefa	$\bar{1}.04$	0.37	0.64	1.48	$\bar{0}.05$
48.	Kullo-Konta	$\bar{1}.51$	0.53	$\bar{0}.12$	1.19	$\bar{1}.20$
49.	Limu	1.11	1.33	0.92	1.64	0.52
50.	Maji and Goldeya	1.41	3.03	$\bar{0}.80$	1.33	$\bar{1}.49$
51.	Chebo and Guraghe	0.09	2.44	0.47	0.52	0.25
52.	Haiqoch and Buttajira	0.71	0.37	0.26	0.39	0.81
53.	Jibat and Mecha	$\bar{1}.28$	0.75	0.67	0.87	1.09
54.	Kembata and Hadiyya	0.35	$\bar{0}.55$	$\bar{0}.16$	0.54	$\bar{0}.63$
55.	Mennaghesha	$\bar{0}.71$	2.03	6.78	0.50	1.95
56.	Menz and Ghishe	$\bar{0}.73$	$\bar{0}.54$	$\bar{0}.57$	0.49	$\bar{1}.49$
57.	Merhabate	0.87	0.04	$\bar{0}.03$	0.68	$\bar{1}.77$
58.	Selale	0.13	1.76	0.76	.67	0.23
59.	Tegulet and Bulga	0.33	1.07	0.52	0.29	1.38
60.	Yerer and Kerreyu	0.83	3.07	1.59	$\bar{0}.11$	1.66
61.	Yifat and Timuga	0.99	$\bar{0}.02$	$\bar{0}.15$	0.17	$\bar{0}.05$
62.	Arero	1.33	$\bar{1}.22$	$\bar{0}.60$	$\bar{1}.07$	$\bar{0}.34$
63.	Ghidewo	$\bar{1}.51$	1.30	1.26	0.50	0.81
64.	Jemjem	$\bar{0}.27$	$\bar{0}.37$	$\bar{0}.41$	$\bar{0}.17$	0.52
65.	Awasa	$\bar{1}.05$	0.51	1.24	0,55	1.38
66.	Welayita	$\bar{0}.47$	$\bar{0}.84$	$\bar{0}.57$	0.51	1.09
67.	Borena	1.64	$\bar{0}.06$	$\bar{0}.99$	$\bar{1}.21$	0.81
68.	Adwa	1.08	$\bar{1}.16$	$\bar{0}.66$	$\bar{0}.99$	0.81
69.	Agame	1.08	$\bar{1}.38$	$\bar{0}.71$	$\bar{1}.26$	0.52
70.	Axum	1.08	$\bar{0}.93$	$\bar{0}.65$	$\bar{0}.63$	0.23
71.	Inderta	1.64	$\bar{0}.73$	0.08	$\bar{1}.21$	1.09
72.	Hulet-Awlailo	1.32	$\bar{1}.57$	$\bar{0}.59$	$\bar{1}.65$	$\bar{1}.20$
73.	Rayya and Azebo	1.47	$\bar{0}.63$	$\bar{0}.34$	$\bar{1}.16$	$\bar{0}.34$
74.	Shire	0.84	$\bar{0}.35$	$\bar{0}.40$	$\bar{0}.40$	$\bar{0}\text{-}34$
75.	Tembien	1.21	$\bar{0}.44$	0.52	$\bar{0}.46$	$\bar{0}.91$
76.	Arjo	$\bar{1}.34$	$\bar{0}.18$	0.03	1.43	$\bar{1}.20$
77.	Asosa	0.07	$\bar{0}.31$	$\bar{0}.24$	0.37	0.34
78.	Ghimbi	$\bar{0}.88$	0.55	1.81	1.10	0.81
79.	Hero-Gudirru	$\bar{1}.51$	0,59	1.30	1.38	$\bar{0}.05$
80.	Qellem	0.45	1.02	1.16	0.80	0.52
81.	Leqa	$\bar{0}.77$	0.27	0.62	1.44	1.38
82.	Ambassel	1.25	$\bar{1}.41$	$\bar{0}.64$	$\bar{0}.70$	0.05
83.	Awsa	2.61	$\bar{1}.22$	$\bar{0}.81$	$\bar{1}.63$	$\bar{0}.05$
84.	Dese-Zuria	0.74	$\bar{0}.52$	$\bar{0}.22$	0.27	1.38
85.	Qallu	0.74	0.14	$\bar{0}.38$	0.17	0.23
86.	Lasta	1.73	$\bar{0}.89$	$\bar{0}.66$	$\bar{0}.10$	$\bar{0}.63$
87.	Rayya and Qobbo	0.74	$\bar{0}.48$	$\bar{0}.16$	$\bar{1}.07$	$\bar{0}.05$

No.	Name of Awraja	FI	SI	CI	FI	DI
88.	Wadla-Delanta	0.30	$\bar{0}$.92	$\bar{0}$.78	0.30	$\bar{1}$.20
89.	Wag	1.84	$\bar{0}$.81	$\bar{0}$.57	$\bar{0}$.57	$\bar{0}$.63
90.	Werre-Himeno	0.30	$\bar{1}$.02	$\bar{0}$.65	0.30	$\bar{1}$.20
91.	Werre-Ilu	0.14	$\bar{0}$.73	$\bar{0}$.84	0.27	$\bar{1}$.20
92.	Yejju	0.92	$\bar{0}$.83	$\bar{0}$.66	$\bar{0}$.66	$\bar{0}$.34
93.	Borena-Sayint	0.07	1.50	$\bar{0}$.87	0.47	$\bar{0}$.91
94.	Hamasen	$\bar{0}$.43	$\bar{0}$.09	1.36	$\bar{0}$.81	1.95
95.	Serae	$\bar{0}$.20	0.17	$\bar{0}$.02	$\bar{0}$.79	1.09
96.	Akeleguzay	0.48	$\bar{0}$.52	$\bar{0}$.13	$\bar{1}$.17	1.09
97.	Keren	0.03	$\bar{0}$.60	$\bar{0}$.36	$\bar{1}$.28	1.38
98.	Aqordat	0.55	$\bar{0}$.29	$\bar{0}$.85	$\bar{1}$.35	0.81
99.	Sahil	$\bar{0}$.33	$\bar{1}$.44	$\bar{1}$.09	$\bar{1}$.89	$\bar{1}$.49
100.	Red-Sea	0.48	$\bar{0}$.97	$\bar{0}$.97	$\bar{1}$.59	1.38
101.	Asab	0.86	$\bar{1}$.28	$\bar{1}$.02	$\bar{1}$.90	0.81
102.	Gash and Setit	0.55	$\bar{0}$.37	$\bar{0}$.83	$\bar{1}$.25	0.23

commercialization and environmental quality. Farm commercialization develops where it pays, that is, where the environmental quality provides the basic incentives. That both subsistence level and farm commercialization are directly related to environmental quality clearly indicates the importance and the influence of the physical environment in rural Ethiopia.

The fact that the highest degree of relationship exists between farm commercialization, on one hand, and environmental quality, famine, subsistence level and level of development respectively, on the other hand, shows the importance and the many-sided effects of farm commercialization.

We are now, it seems, on much better ground to emphasize that the subsistence production system is the root of famine, and that the persistent oppressions and exploitation of peasants by socio-economic and political forces rather than the occasional aberrations of the natural forces are the decisive factors of vulnerability to famine.

We can also state more emphatically the urgent need for a development policy that is committed to welfare of the masses of Ethiopian peasants. If the so-called development serves only to provide access to the various instruments of oppression and exploitation into the rural areas in order to maximize "the irreducible claims of outsiders" before the subsistence requirements of the peasants are ensured, famine will continue to haunt rural Ethiopia.

NOTES

[1]TBU is Tropical Bovine Unit calculated as follows:

    1 TBU = one animal weighing 250 kgs. for 60% of bovine herd, horses, and camels

                = younger, remaining 40%, 2 herds
                = 10 sheep
                = 10 goats
                = 2 donkeys

See U.N. Conference on Desertification, *Ecological Change and Desertification*, August 29—September 9, 1977, Nairobi.

[2]We have taken the 102 *awrajas* to be a population rather than a sample. See Maurice G. Kendall and Alan Stuart, *The Advanced Theory of Statistics* (London, 1967), Vol 2, pp. 536-47.

PART V

CONCLUSIONS

Chapter Eight

Conclusion

We have rejected those conception and explanations that externalize the factors that generate famine. Such conceptions and explanations of famine cloud our understanding of the problem. Moreover, by removing the issues out of the real context of famine, the famine-prone society itself, these views tend to delay resolute action by exaggerating external forces and underestimating the responsibility of internal socio-economic and political forces.

We have, on the contrary, been emphasizing the role of the internal forces in famine, a role that both by commission and omission is decisive in the propagation of famine. This study has attempted to demonstrate that the subsistence production system, with its incapacitating disincentives of oppression and exploitation. which keeps peasants and their families permanently at barely subsistence level without any means of averting or of coping with the consequences of crop failure, is the system that creates famine in time of peace. A subsistence production system impoverishes peasants and pastoralists as well as the physical environment. It is this fact that occasionally disturbs the delicate balance between the activities and expectations of the peasants and pastoralists, on one hand, and the process of the physical environment, on the other. When this delicate balance is disturbed, famine does not occur automatically, but instead takes several months to mature into a mass killer. Social irresponsibility first creates a delicate balance between subsistence producers and the physical environment; then it disturbs this balance by insatiable greed; and then allows the process of famine to proceed unchecked to full maturity.

The evidence shows that the quality of the physical environment is very important. Famine is associated with deficiencies in the physical environment. But deficiencies in the physical environment are a way of expressing human limitations rather than objective conditions. What we call the deficiencies of the physical environment are only reflections of some thwarted human desires and hopes. Without thwarted human purposes, there are no deficiencies in the physical environment.

How many years of experience does it take to recognize the deficiencies of the physical environment which, as we said, are human limitations? How many generations does it take to learn from the pain and agony of famine and to master the physical environment? This question will lead us to another age-old question: Is it possible for any society to master the physical environment, if it has not developed the organizational and technological competence to master itself?

The physical environment presents itself as it is; no more, no less. It is society that ought to learn and constantly reduce its limitations with respect to the physical environment. Famine is a consequence of the failure to learn from the constant interactions between a society and its physical environment. In these constant interactions the burden of adjustment is on society, not on the physical environment. Famine is a human responsibility.

Once the society as a whole and the ruling elite in particular accept the ultimate responsibility for the process of famine and its consequences, famine can be prevented. The task may appear to be formidable. But wherever a society is organized and directed democratically by a sense of social responsibility and accountability, there can be no alternative to accepting the challenge of famine.[1] Given either one of two conditions, famine need not happen: either the social system must enable peasants to produce above their subsistence requirements and to take the responsibility for maintaining adequate reserves of cash and grain for emergency purposes; or, alternatively, the government must take the responsibility for maintaining sufficient reserves of food supply, especially in those parts of the country where the probability of crop failure appears to be relatively high. These conditions are based on a very simple and natural tendency that is characteristic even of some lower animals. It is at a time of plenty that a society has to call upon its capability of anticipating future scarcity and of setting aside essential provisions for such an eventuality. No peasant will fail to understand such simple mechanisms of self-preservation, especially if he is allowed to have that mechanism under his control. Bitter experience has taught Ethiopian peasants to regard any apparent good intention of government with suspicion.

When a problem is properly identified, the solution suggests itself automatically. Consequently, our identification of famine as an inherent characteristic of subsistence production system suggests certain actions that can be taken to eradicate the threat of famine. In general, simultaneous action is needed on all the three elements of subsistence production system, namely, the natural forces, the peasant world, and the socio-economic and political forces. To put it differently, famine can be prevented by taking certain measures to control harmful natural forces, or to have sufficient reserves of food and cash in order to reduce their harmful effects; by allowing the peasant masses to articulate their own problems and priorities, and by restoring to them their self-confidence and self-respect in order to mobilize their energy and resources to improve their own conditions of living; and by tightly controlling the governmental and market forces through a responsible and responsive administrative structure in which the peasants should actively and decisively participate.

In spite of their contradictions and their doubtful merit, prescriptions for rural development abound. What is frequently lacking is not so much ideas or techniques as the will and the commitment to improve the socio-economic condition of undemanding peasants. In this connection it may be necessary to mention two pitfalls that must be avoided. First and foremost, no nation can afford to abdicate the pain of thinking in order to identify its own problems, to consider alternative remedies, and to work out priorities for them. Perhaps the root of so-called underdevelopment is an aversion to the pain of thinking and the effortless inclination to look for untested prescriptions for vaguely comprehended problems. The pain of thinking can replace the pain of famine.

The second pitfall is the adoption of veterinarian-type prescriptions for the problems of underdevelopment in general. The veterinarian does not have the advantage (or, perhaps, the disadvantage) of a patient that can articulate his ailment: it is this lack of articulation on the part of a specific people that makes veterinarian-type prescriptions at best useless. The necessity of taking into account the peculiar characteristics of the physical environment and the special socio-psychological qualities of the people cannot be ignored without grave consequences. Espeically for a complex country like Ethiopia, the objection to general prescriptions must be instituted as a basic rule in planning. Farming in Agame is not the same thing as farming in Chilalo, nor is farming in Tegulet and Bulga the same thing as farming in Kefa; nor is nomadic pastoralism in Warder the same thing as in Chercher and Adal and Gara Gurracha. That Elkerre *Awraja*, with a river on either side of it, had 13 famine years out of 20 is a peculiar condition that merits special investigation. Similarly, that Bunno Beddelle, situated in the wettest region of the country, is a famine-prone island calls for closer examination. How do we explain the fact that Yerer and Kerreyu *Awraja*, which has the highest concentration of power production, a number of important industries, and large-scale commercial farms, is famine-prone? These are only a few examples that demonstrate our objection to veterinarian-type prescriptions.

In line with the arguments outlined above, we shall refrain from providing general prescriptions. Instead, we shall limit ourselves to structural changes that may create favourable conditions for removing the threat of famine from all parts of rural Ethiopia. We shall discuss these suggestions under the following headings: The problem of Data; Research and development; Administrative Reforms; Taxation.

The Problem of Data

At the most elementary level, the value of data collection, classification and storage is something that is not yet recognized by most ministries, departments and other institutions of government. There are 14 *kifle haghers* or administrative regions, 102 *awrajas* or provinces, and 588 *weredas* or districts. So far the only data that are available at the *wereda* level are those of the Ministry of Public Health. Even at the *awraja* level, such ministries as those of Agriculture, Industry, Finance, and the Interior do not have any data. Most government departments find it easy to deal with aggregates at the *kifle hagher* level, One cannot, for instance, find any data on the number of tractors, amount of fertilizers used, or even the number of agricultural extension agents, by *awraja*. Fortunately, however, the Central Statistical Office is beginning to recognize the usefulness of aggregating data at least by *awraja*. This is true only for data collected by the Central Statistical Office itself and not for data acquired from the ministries and other government departments. That this country has never had any census is the most obvious sign of the failure to recognize the value of accurate information.

Even when institutions exist primarily for the collection and dissemination of data, such as the Climatological Institute, utter misconceptions of their role prevent them from rendering the essential service of providing accurate data. It may sound an exaggeration to say that often even climatological information is treated like a very sensitive state secret. Any person who has ever found it necessary to approach the Climatological Institute for data has to go through a laborious system of red tape. The problem, therefore, is not only the lack of data at a lower level of aggregation, there is also the problem of access to available information. Individuals or institutions that wish to do research are constricted by the problem of the quantity and quality of data they may have to use. This is a very serious handicap that the revolutionary government must remove before it can contemplate any serious planning.

Research and Development

There is hardly any doubt that development-oriented research is basic both to identifying problems and to finding solutions for them; yet neither is there much doubt that development-oriented research is one of the most neglected activities in Ethiopia. If one can talk of research at all in Ethiopia, it is both haphazard and inconsequential. It is haphazard because it is conducted by individuals on the basis of their personal interests and inclinations; and it is inconsequential because it lacks practicability as well as audience at the crucial level of authority. This is, of course, to be expected, because, had the government offices been interested in research at all, they would have first demonstrated it by giving value to information collection, classification, and storage. Dearth of data and disinterest in serious research are compensated by hastily concocted reports which turn into plans. How many five-year plans did Ethiopia have? Decisions based on such hastily drawn up plans and projects may be as fruitless as they are costly. They only sustain the bureaucracy and allow it to muddle through.

But muddling through cannot be a substitute for painful thinking.

It only postpones the real issues and nagging problem until they become unbearable. When the accumulated problems explode and demand not only recognition but also immediate solution—that is to say, when the insensitivity and inefficiency of muddling through is exposed,—once again the pain of thinking is replaced by the energy of emotional reactions. Muddling through, therefore, cannot provide a rational solution to social, economic and political problems. It is, in fact, a mechanism for delaying rational solutions.

The need for systematic research on the physical environment, including climate, soil, slope, and underground water as well as on water conservation methods has never been as pressing as it is at present. For a poor country like Ethiopia, it is imperative to have a complete inventory of its resources which can supply a basis for any meaningful research. Equally important is the establishment of a closer working relationship between government officials who make decisions and the researchers in various institutions. Certainly the Institute of Development Research has never had any impact on the government. It is doubtful how much influence the Institute of Agricultural Research has had on the formulation of agricultural policy.

The University as a whole has yet to be used by other government institutions for any serious research with logical results. We shall presently suggest at least one possible area of cooperation between governmental administration and the University.

Administrative Reform

It has been emphasized earlier that the basic source of rural infirmity is the disorganization of the rural population. One of the most significant gains of the rural population from the Ethiopian Revolution is the organization of the peasants into associations. These peasant associations are further organized into large groups at *wereda, awraja, kifle hagher* and national levels. These peasant associations can play a major role in the rural transformation of Ethiopia, provided they are allowed to take the initiative for, and to be the leading agents of, that transformation. The structural changes in the form of peasant associations brought about by the revolution, although a very significant step forward, can be useful and lasting only when the peasants derive material benefits from them.

TABLE XXI

NUMBER AND SIZE OF MEMBERS OF FARMERS' ASSOCIATIONS BY
Kifle Hager, 1981

Kifle Hagher	No. of Farmers' Associations	No. of Members
Illubabor	980	198,546
Eritrea	281	60,750
Kefa	1645	535,474
Wello	1703	1,022,482
Wellega	2210	449,792
Gamo Gofa	777	211,976
Gonder	1137	427,209
Gojjam	1920	456,242
Arsi	1119	290,000
Harrerghe	1608	420,957
Sidamo	1482	601,043
Shewa	6044	1,703,662
Bale	696	170,000
Tigray	1064	499,076
Total	22666	7,047,209
Average	1619	503,372

Source: Ministry of Agriculture, February 1981.

In order to augment the peasant associations and to turn them into an effective instrument for rural change, a decisive and institutional rearrangement of the administrative system appears to be essential. The major objectives of administrative reorganization may be to create all the necessary conditions to raise the productivity and the standard of living of the rural population, to boost the self-confidence of the peasants, and to make them masters of their own destiny. Three principal directions of change may be visualized: first, the rearrangement of *awraja* boundaries; second, the replacement of bureaucratic administrators by specially trained creative agents of change; and third, the institution of an administrative mechanism which permits a wider involvement and a decisive participation of peasants.

The existing administrative divisions have no rational basis, and often become a very serious inconvenience to social and economic development, as well as to administrative efficiency. It may be useful, therefore, to recognize the *awrajas* into manageable sizes, taking into account population and land resources as major factors. In addition, it may be necessary to do away with the cumbersome and purely bureaucratic division of the *kifle hagher*. For administrative purposes, the country may be simply divided into *awrajas* and *weredas*, the latter constituting a certain number of peasant associations which may vary from place to place.

For both levels of administration (*awraja* and *wereda*), the selection of a new breed of administrators who possess the requisite qualities for generating change in rural Ethiopia, and of training such managers of change who will be equal to the hard task and responsibility, is a desideratum. For too long, the rural people of Ethiopia have been the victims of perhaps well-meaning but ill-advised tyrants of every kind. They are tired of being told about their problems by administrators who never felt these problems. They are tired of being told about solutions that have little relevance to their real and nagging problems. They are tired of raising money from projects that never materialize. The new breed of administrators must be made to understand this psychological exhaustion of the rural population. It is not administrators with a presumption of knowing all the problems and unfounded confidence in having ready-made solutions, not administrators who are so totally possessed by their enthusiasm for action that they have no time to reflect on the reality that confronts them—it is not administrators armed with textbook solutions for textbook problems that are needed. It is, rather, administrators who realize that the problems are yet to be encountered, to be identified, to be studied, and to be analysed in the specific contexts of assignment with the active assistance and participation of the local inhabitants.

The world of underdevelopment is a world of faith as opposed to critical reason. The rural population of Ethiopia is the best representative of that world of faith. The new administrators may find it necessary to understand this fact thoroughly, and their training ought to provide them with a large measure of faith to direct critical reason and a large measure of critical reason to purge faith first in themselves. In their dealings with the peasant world, too, they need to understand the power of faith to relate to rural people, and critical reason to be effective in the ultimate objective of their assignment, which is to change the rural society's outlook and direct it towards a scientific path. They ought to be convinced that their task will be easier if they start not by attacking faith but by enlarging the people's capacity for critical reason, so that they themselves will purge their faith.

It is idle to expect the rural people of Ethiopia to cooperate whole-heartedly in a plan or project that they rightly or wrongly believe is outside the realm of their pressing needs. In such instances, they can only become passive spectators, or, at the most, reluctant participants who will forget the whole thing as soon as the pressure is off them. This is why it is necessary for the new administrators to work with the people by allowing them a large measure of involvement in identifying problems, in setting priorities, in allocating resources, and in deciding the course of action. If the rural people share the responsibility for the administration of development, the government may discover that no sacrifice will be too much for them as long as they remain convinced that they are the ultimate beneficiaries.

It appears that the only way of removing even the threat of oppression and exploitation is to make administrators accountable not only to the government that selects; trains, and appoints them, but also to the people whom they are required to serve. The provision of some institutional framework that will enable the people periodically to assess and to control the administration is a crucial aspect of the administrative reorganization.

The University may play a vital role in the training of administrators for both *awraja* and *wereda* levels. The courses have to avoid the beaten track and chart a new avenue that will lead to the desired objectives. This training process may be conducted so creatively and imaginatively that what is ultimately expected from the trainees is demonstrated in practical terms to them.

Taxation

Without involving ourselves in unnecessary consideration of the principles of taxation, we may start by accepting that "a tax is a compulsory contribution imposed by a public authority, irrespective of the exact amount of service rendered to the tax payer in return, and not imposed as a penalty for any legal offense".[2] In its entirety, this definition fits the Ethiopian rural situation with regard to taxation. The rural people acquired hardly anything in return for the land tax, agricultural income tax, education tax, and health tax they were former ly to pay.

The concentration of opportunities in the towns leaves the rural areas in atrophy. The two most urbanized Governorate Generals, Eritrea and Shewa, together with the city of Addis Ababa, have the lion's share of all the opportunities for development. That 68.7% of the total number of teachers in both elementary and secondary schools are found in Addis Ababa, Eritrea and Shewa shows the malady that is elephantiasis. As a result 45.6% of the children in elementary schools and 63.6% of those in the secondary are concentrated in the same areas. Similarly these favoured areas command the services of 45.5% of the hospitals, 47.8% of the clinics, 74.0% of the doctors and 87.3% of the nurses. Lest some miss the point, this is not merely concentration of facilities, it is rather a concentration of causes, the gods, that created these facilities. It is a concentration of power and wealth. It represents insatiable greed and blind exploitation.[3]

In such a situation, taxation becomes only legalized exploitation. Moreover, when peasants are forced to pay taxes even when their gross production is insufficient to meet their subsistence requirements, taxation turns into a brutal form of legalized exploitation. Sometimes arguments are advanced to justify agricultural taxation as an inducement to higher productivity, without considering the problem of subsistence.[4]

The point that we are stressing is articulated by Galbraith:

In the strategy of modern development, taxation—what has come to be called fiscal savings—plays a considerable role. In the less developed land, there is also some likelihood that taxation will fall rather heavily on the poor who, after all, are available in the most abundant supply. And since the underdeveloped country is, *pro tanto*, an agricultural community, there may be a traditional tendency for this taxation to fall upon the farmer or his land. Thus, not only does undifferentiated growth tend to support higher income consumption, it may do so partly as the result of saving from lower income consumption.[5]

This is obviously something that the revolutionary government cannot allow to continue. Ultimately, when famine occurs, the cost of relief will dwarf any revenue acquired by taxing the rural population. It may be reasonable, therefore, to suggest the suspension of taxation in cash in all the famine-prone *awrajas*.[6] In these *awrajas*, peasants may pay taxes in the form of labour input in development projects of their own. Such a moratorium on taxation may, on one hand, allow the people to build some reserves, and, on the other, encourage the development of the necessary infrastructure by using the surplus labour.

With some government assistance, the labour in lieu of taxation can be used for numerous development projects such as reafforestation, water conservation, irrigation, housing, road construction, or any other need that the people give priority to. Perhaps a very desirable side-effect of substituting cash taxation by labour for a recognized social purpose may be that it demonstrates to the rural population the benefits of cooperation and of socializing work. The payment of tax in cash is an individual act based on individual differences of land-holding or income and, therefore, an act that affirms individualism. But tax payment in form of labour introduces "social activity and social mind".[7] Rural regeneration and development can become a reality only by first giving the rural people the opportunity to regain confidence both in themselves and in government officials. A moratorium on taxation in the famine-prone regions will undoubtedly help to reestablish mutual confidence between the government and the rural population and clear the way for a more fruitful and closer cooperation to remove the threat of famine from Ethiopia.

No government can be free from responsibility for famine that decimates its population, all good intentions notwithstanding. The rural people who have the bitter experience of famine and who are the potential victims of future famine must be given the chance to think and plan for themselves by removing all burdens from them and by allowing them to share in the responsibility for the future. That may prove to be a firm foundation for social reconstruction in rural Ethiopia.

NOTES

[1]A very interesting case was brought to my attention by the people in the University Famine Relief and Rehabilitation Organization. Rayya and Qobbo *Awraja* was one of the hardest hit *awrajas* in Wello. We now learn that a village

called Mendefera in Rayya and Qobbo was not at all affected by the famine that commenced in that *awarja* in 1972. The people of that village did not take any relief aid. How did this village remain an island in the midst of terrible famine? Although it is too early yet to state the exact reasons, it appears that the village is noted for two characteristics, a very tight organization with a rather stiff hierarchy and ferocity in demanding respect for its rights.

[2]Hugh Dalton, *Principles of Public Finance*, (London, 1966), p. 23.

[3]Mesfin Wolde-Mariam, *Rural-Urban Split, op. cit.*, pp. 11-12.

[4]See, for instance, Taye Gulilat, "The Tax in Lieu of Tithe and the New Agricultural Income Tax: A Preliminary Evaluation", *Dialogue*, a Publication of Ethiopian University Teachers Association (Addis Ababa, December, 1968), Vol. II, No. 1, pp. 17-27.

[5]7ohn Kenneth Galbraith, *Economic Development, op. cit.*, p. 7.

[6]Apparently this is not a novel idea. In Vietnam the Vietcong set a limit for "the untaxable minimum" subsistence requirement. See Colin Clark and Margaret Haswell, *The Economics of Subsistence Agriculture*, (Glasgow, 1970), p. 58.

[7]Karl Marx, *Economic and Philosophic Manuscripts, op. cit.*, p. 137.

Index